GOD'S MASTERWORK

A Concerto in Sixty-Six Movements

Volume One

Genesis through Second Chronicles

From the Bible-teaching ministry of

CHARLES R. SWINDOLL

INSIGHT FOR LIVING

Chuck graduated in 1963 from Dallas Theological Seminary, where he now serves as the school's fourth president, helping to prepare a new generation of men and women for the ministry. Chuck has served in pastorates in three states: Massachusetts, Texas, and California, including almost twenty-three years at the First Evangelical Free Church in Fullerton, California. His sermon messages have been aired over radio since 1979 as the *Insight for Living* broadcast. A best-selling author, Chuck has written numerous books and booklets on many subjects.

Based on the outlines and transcripts of Chuck's sermons, the study guide text is co-authored by Gary Matlack, a graduate of Texas Tech University and Dallas Theological Seminary. He also wrote the Living Insights sections.

Editor in Chief:
Cynthia Swindoll

Coauthor of Text:
Gary Matlack

Assistant Editor and Writer:
Wendy Peterson

Copy Editors:
Tom Kimber
Marco Salazar

Cover Designer:
Nina Paris

Text Designer:
Gary Lett

Graphics System Administrator:
Bob Haskins

Publishing System Specialist:
Alex Pasieka

Director, Communications Division:
John Norton

Marketing Manager:
Alene Cooper

Project Coordinator:
Colette Muse

Printer:
Sinclair Printing Company

Unless otherwise identified, all Scripture references are from the New American Standard Bible, © The Lockman Foundation 1960, 1962, 1963, 1968, 1971, 1972, 1973, 1975, 1977. Used by permission. Scripture taken from the Holy Bible, New International Version © 1973, 1978, 1984 International Bible Society, used by permission of Zondervan Bible Publishers.

Series ISBN 0-8499-1474-4—*God's Masterwork: A Concerto in Sixty-Six Movements*

Study guide ISBN 0-8499-8738-5—*Volume One: Genesis–2 Chronicles*

COVER PHOTOGRAPHY: Neo Photo, Inc., Jack Fritze, photographer

COVER BACKGROUND PHOTO: Superstock

CONTENTS

INTRODUCTION

What is my final authority?"

That is a foundational question all of us, especially we who embrace Christ, must answer. Where do we go for a clear understanding of right and wrong? Where do we turn for guidance when we encounter difficult decisions, cultural pressures, and times of personal crises? What source can we consult for the truth about who God is, who we are, and how He has bridged the distance between us?

The psalmist answered this way:

> Thy servant meditates on Thy statutes.
> Thy testimonies also are my delight;
> They are my counselors. (Ps. 119:23b–24)

Make no mistake about it . . . God's Word, the Bible, is our final authority for faith and practice. It is living, infallible truth from our living, infallible God. Knowing and loving Him begins with knowing and loving His Word.

God's Masterwork: A Concerto in Sixty-Six Movements is designed to help you get a handle on the whole of Scripture so you can understand its message more fully . . . and love its Author more deeply.

In this first volume, we'll cover the big picture from Genesis through 2 Chronicles. The names will be familiar to you. Adam. Abraham. Moses. David. But this may be the first time you've seen them all together as part of God's unfolding plan for the ages.

So let's "delight" in God's Word, our final authority, together. And, together, let's delight in Him.

Chuck Swindoll

Chuck Swindoll

PUTTING TRUTH
INTO ACTION

K nowledge apart from application falls short of God's desire for
His children. He wants us to apply what we learn so that we
will change and grow. This study guide was prepared with these
goals in mind. As you go through the following pages, we hope your
desire to discover biblical truth will grow as your understanding of
God's Word increases and that you will be encouraged to apply what
you've learned.

To assist you in your study, we've included a section called
Living Insights at the end of each lesson. These exercises will
challenge you to study further and to think of specific ways to put
your discoveries into action.

On occasion a lesson is followed by a **Digging Deeper** section, which gives you additional information and resources to probe
further into some issues raised in that lesson.

There are many ways to use this guide—in personal devotions,
group studies, discussions with friends and family, and Sunday school
classes. And, of course, it's an ideal study aid when you're listening
to its corresponding *Insight for Living* radio series.

To benefit most from this study guide, we would encourage you
to consider it a spiritual journal. That's why we've included space
in the **Living Insights** for recording your thoughts and discoveries.
We hope you'll return to those sections often for review and encouragement as you continue to grow in your walk with Christ.

Gary Matlack

Gary Matlack
Coauthor of Text
Author of Living Insights

GOD'S MASTERWORK

A Concerto in Sixty-Six Movements

Volume One

Genesis through Second Chronicles

SURVEY CHART OF THE BIBLE BOOKS

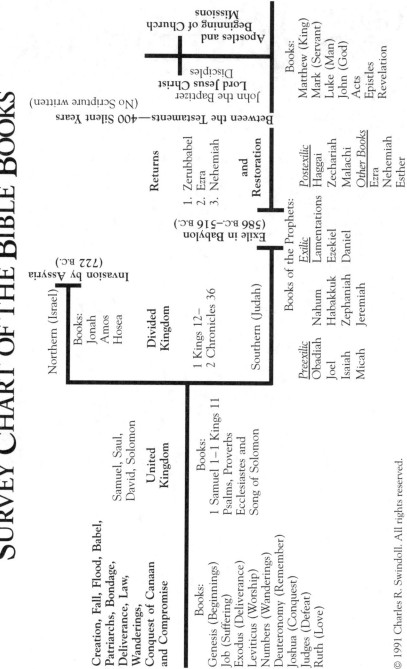

Apostles and Beginning of Church Missions

Books:
Matthew (King)
Mark (Servant)
Luke (Man)
John (God)
Acts
Epistles
Revelation

John the Baptizer Lord Jesus Christ Disciples

Between the Testaments—400 Silent Years (No Scripture written)

Returns

1. Zerubbabel
2. Ezra
3. Nehemiah

and Restoration

Postexilic
Haggai
Zechariah
Malachi
Other Books
Ezra
Nehemiah
Esther

Exile in Babylon (586 B.C.–516 B.C.)

Exilic
Lamentations
Ezekiel
Daniel

Invasion by Assyria (722 B.C.)

Northern (Israel)

Books:
Jonah
Amos
Hosea

Divided Kingdom

1 Kings 12–
2 Chronicles 36

Southern (Judah)

Books of the Prophets:

Preexilic
Obadiah
Joel
Isaiah
Micah

Nahum
Habakkuk
Zephaniah
Jeremiah

Creation, Fall, Flood, Babel,
Patriarchs, Bondage,
Deliverance, Law,
Wanderings,
Conquest of Canaan
and Compromise

Samuel, Saul,
David, Solomon

United Kingdom

Books:
Genesis (Beginnings)
Job (Suffering)
Exodus (Deliverance)
Leviticus (Worship)
Numbers (Wanderings)
Deuteronomy (Remember)
Joshua (Conquest)
Judges (Defeat)
Ruth (Love)

Books:
1 Samuel 1–1 Kings 11
Psalms, Proverbs
Ecclesiastes and
Song of Solomon

Chapter 1

A SYMPHONY FOR THE SOUL

Selected Scriptures

Ahhh, that's beautiful. Can you hear it? The Bible, that is. What a masterfully orchestrated piece, a symphony for the soul. You have to listen closely and let it all soak in to really appreciate it. The highs, the lows. The peaceful interludes, the thundering crescendos.

Oh. You never thought of the Bible as a piece of music? Well, technically it's not. But the similarities are intriguing. Any musical masterpiece, for example, will endure for years, even centuries, beyond the date of its writing. Handel's *Messiah*, first performed in 1742, stills moves audiences today. The classic works of Bach, Beethoven, and Mozart, once played in royal courts, cathedrals, and concert halls can now be listened to in the comfort of your living room.

Likewise, the Bible stands unruffled by the winds of time. And like all great compositions, the Bible has its critics.

Critics Who Have Come and Gone

In A.D. 303, for instance, the emperor Diocletian issued an edict to stop Christians from worshiping and to destroy their Scriptures. Twenty-five years later, Constantine, who succeeded Diocletian, ordered copies of the Scriptures to be prepared at the government's expense.[1]

---

1. Josh McDowell, comp., *Evidence That Demands a Verdict*, rev. ed. (San Bernardino, Calif.: Here's Life Publishers, 1979), p. 20.

The French philosopher Voltaire announced that in one hundred years from his time, Christianity would be swept from existence. Ironically, only fifty years after Voltaire's death, the Geneva Bible Society used his press and house to produce stacks of Bibles.[2]

"A thousand times over," said Bernard Ramm, "the death knell of the Bible has been sounded, the funeral procession formed, the inscription cut on the tombstone, and committal read. But somehow the corpse never stays put."[3]

Diocletian, Voltaire, and countless other critics of the Bible are now mere whispers from history. But the symphony of Scripture plays on.

The Bible has sold more copies and has been translated into more languages than any other piece of literature. A work of such prevailing truth deserves to be pored over and appreciated. And that's the reason for this study. After you complete this five-part series, you will have an overview of the entire Bible, God's masterwork. Then you'll have on your shelf a framework for a lifetime of exploration. Let's start, then, with some general information about this splendid symphony of Scripture.

General Information

The Bible, like any great work of music, has a title, structural divisions, a history, and a main theme.

The Title

You will not find our word *Bible* anywhere in Scripture. Surprised? Even more surprising is that the name actually comes from the Greek word for the papyrus plant, *biblos*. Christians as early as the second century A.D. were using the plural form, *biblia*, when referring to their writings. And the word kept traveling through Latin and on into Old French, until it finally reached English and became *Bible*.[4]

Though it is a collection of many books by many different authors, the Bible can rightly be called one book since it has one heavenly Author—God—and one main message.

2. McDowell, *Evidence That Demands a Verdict*, p. 20.

3. McDowell, *Evidence That Demands a Verdict*, p. 21.

4. See Norman L. Geisler and William E. Nix, A *General Introduction to the Bible*, rev. ed. (Chicago, Ill.: Moody Press, 1986), p. 21.

The Divisions

Any great musical composition has structure—deliberate organization that enhances the development and presentation of the whole. And so it is with Scripture.

When you open your Bible to the table of contents, you'll notice the two most obvious divisions—the Old and New Testaments. A testament, according to Norman Geisler and William Nix, is a

> "covenant, or compact, or arrangement between two parties." . . . The Old Testament was first called *the* covenant in Moses' day (Ex. 24:8). Later, Jeremiah announced that God would make a "new covenant" with His people (Jer. 31:31–34), which Jesus claimed to do at the Last Supper (Matt. 26:28, cf. 1 Cor. 11:23–25; Heb. 8:6–8). Hence, it is for Christians that the former part of the Bible is called the *Old* Covenant (Testament), and the latter is called the *New* Covenant.[5]

Saint Augustine related the two testaments this way: "The Old Testament revealed in the New, the New veiled in the Old."[6] The Old Testament foreshadows Christ, while the New Testament presents Him in all His fullness. For example, the sacrificial system detailed in Leviticus pictures the necessity of sacrifice in order for sinful humanity to fellowship with a holy God. But in the book of Matthew, we actually see Christ suffer and die for the sins of the world. Leviticus, then, as well as all the Old Testament, presents the atoning death of Christ in pictures and shadows. The New Testament presents Him in person and substance.

The thirty-nine books of the Old Testament can be further categorized into four groups.

Old Testament

- *Legal* (Genesis through Deuteronomy): These first five books of the Old Testament, penned by Moses, focus on God's requirements for right living, which are most clearly seen in the Mosaic Law.

- *Historical* (Joshua through Esther): The next twelve books trace

---

5. Geisler and Nix, *A General Introduction to the Bible*, pp. 21–22.

6. Geisler and Nix, *A General Introduction to the Bible*, p. 22.

the development, disobedience, downfall, and deliverance of God's people, the nation Israel.

- *Poetical* (Job through Song of Solomon): Beginning with the laments of Job, we move to the psalmists' praise and pleas to Solomon's words of wisdom. The power of God's Spirit to move people's hearts is perhaps more evident in the five poetical books than in any other section of Scripture.

- *Prophetical* (Isaiah through Malachi): The prophets called God's people to righteous living and foretold His judgment on those who turned their backs on Him. Isaiah through Daniel make up the Major Prophets, simply because they are the longest prophetic books. Hosea through Malachi, shorter prophetic books, are considered the Minor Prophets.[7]

God certainly has an appreciation for diversity! Rather than dumping raw information on us, He revealed Himself in a way that preserved all the drama and beauty of history.

Now, on to the New Testament. Its twenty-seven books also subdivide into four sections.

New Testament

- *Biographical* (Matthew through John): The four gospels, each written to a different audience, play out the life, death, and resurrection of our Savior. Each gospel gives a slightly different perspective. Matthew presents Jesus as the long-awaited Messiah, the King of the Jews. Mark sees Him as the consummate Servant. Luke the physician reveals Him as the compassionate Son of Man. And John gives us a glimpse into the eternal existence of the Son of God.

- *Historical* (Acts): The book of Acts provides us with an unfolding narrative of the Gospels' expansion and the birth and growth of the church.

- *Doctrinal* (Romans through Jude): These are also called the Epistles, or letters. Paul wrote thirteen (fourteen if you include

---

7. J. Sidlow Baxter further clarifies this distinction: "The twelve writings grouped as the 'Minor Prophets,' though they amplify various aspects, do not determine the main shape of Messianic prophecy. They conform to the general frame already formed for us in Isaiah, Jeremiah, Ezekiel and Daniel." *Explore the Book*, six vols. in one (Grand Rapids, Mich.: Zondervan Publishing House, Academie Books, 1966), p. 200.

Hebrews). The rest came from the pens of James, Peter, John, and Jude. Each letter lays out a carefully thought-through treatment of theological truth. They are essays, in a sense, that apply the gospel to everyday life.

- *Prophetical* (Revelation): Through the holy vision of John, the book of Revelation transports us to the end times, when Christ will return to earth in glory, judgment, and power.

THE BIBLE

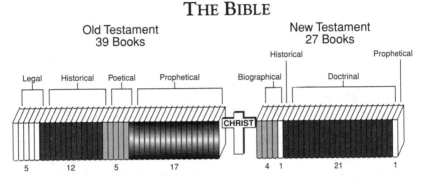

That's a quick look at how the Bible is organized. Now let's see how it came to us.

The History

The sixty-six books of the Bible were written over a period of 1500 years by more than forty people, who came from all walks of life. The Bible covers the whole span of history, from the creation of the heavens and the earth to their re-creation into the new heavens and new earth. It is a book written by real people about real people, containing actual events and reliable truth.

The Old Testament writers wrote in Hebrew and some Aramaic. The New Testament was recorded in Koine (common) Greek.

How did our Bible come to us in its current form? Good question—whole books have been written to answer it. For our purposes, though, a brief explanation by Geisler and Nix will be helpful:

> There are four links in the chain "from God to us": inspiration, canonization, transmission, and translation. In the first, God gave the message to the prophets who received and recorded it. Canonization, the second link, dealt with the recognition and collection of the prophetic writings. . . . In order for

succeeding generations to share in this revelation the Scriptures had to be copied, translated, recopied, and retranslated. This process not only provided the Scriptures for other nations, but for other generations as well. [This] third link is known as transmission. . . .

A translation is simply the rendering of a given composition from one language into another.[8]

The Bible has been meticulously copied, translated, and preserved throughout history. So any of the popular English translations we have today—*New International Version*, *New American Standard Bible*, *New King James Version*, etc.—are completely reliable reflections of the original text.

The Theme

Like any great piece of music, the Bible has a main theme running through it: *Salvation through the Lord Jesus Christ.* Wherever you turn, you hear the same melody—God rescuing people from their sin through the atoning death of His own Son. It begins softly in Genesis, then weaves its way through the entire Old Testament. After a lingering silence between the Testaments, it bursts forth in the Gospels and plays steadily throughout the New Testament, building toward a grand finale in Revelation.

Crucial Doctrines

As we seek to understand and trust the reliability of God's Word, we need to keep four crucial doctrines in mind.

Revelation

God chose to give His truth to us—that's revelation; that's how we know Him. If God had kept silent, our souls would have never known Him or the sweet music of His Word.

His revelation comes to us in a variety of ways. First by *illustration*—His masterful work of creation. Though this general revelation of God does not save us, it allows us to see His majesty in the stars, the crash of the waves, the towering redwoods, and the snow-dusted mountains (see Ps. 8). God also *spoke* directly to those who would record His words. Sometimes He spoke directly

8. Geisler and Nix, *A General Introduction to the Bible*, p. 321, 493.

from heaven; other times He sent an angel. He spoke to some through dreams and visions. In Moses' case, He spoke from a burning bush. Some truths, such as the Ten Commandments, were directly written down by God.

Inspiration

Second Timothy 3:16 tells us that "all Scripture is *inspired* by God" (emphasis added). The Greek word literally means "God-breathed." So God breathed out His Word, which was written down by human agents. It's important to see inspiration as more than mere mechanical dictation. God was able to record His exact, inerrant words without destroying the individuality, personality, or literary style of the writers (see also 2 Pet. 1:20–21).

Illumination

Where revelation deals with God's giving of truth and inspiration deals with recording it, illumination addresses the understanding of it. When we read and study the Scriptures, the Author is present through His Holy Spirit, God massages that truth into our hearts and stirs us to action (see John 16:13; 1 Cor. 2:9–16).

Application

Application is the ability to appropriate the Scriptures into daily experience. It's possible to know God's Word and yet not live it. God's truth must churn through our minds, seep into our hearts, and flow out to every area of life. As we study, we need to ask, "Is this true in my life? What do I need to change?" and other questions that prompt us to apply God's truth. Being hearers of the Word, as James says, is not enough. We must be doers of the Word (see James 1:22–25; see also John 13:17).

God has revealed Himself to us. He has recorded His truth and preserved it through the centuries. His Holy Spirit helps us understand it. And it will change our lives. That's music worth listening to.

 Living Insights

> Thy word is a lamp to my feet,
> And a light to my path. (Ps. 119:105)

The psalmist hits on the reason we study the Bible. Why we

discuss it, debate it, and revere it. Because it tells us how to live. It puts us on the path of life by introducing us to Jesus Christ; then it tells us how to walk with Him. Without the Word of God, we would fumble around in the dark.

What areas of your life need more light? This might be a good time to make a list of questions you have or problems you're facing that the Bible can address. As you progress through this series, make note of which books touch on the topics you want to explore. When you complete the series, go back and study the sections of Scripture that deal with your questions.

_____

_____

_____

_____

_____

_____

_____

_____

_____

_____

_____

_____

_____

_____

_____

_____

_____

_____

Chapter 2

GENESIS: WHERE IT ALL BEGINS

A *Survey of Genesis*

Before the mountains were born,
Or Thou didst give birth to the earth and the world,
Even from everlasting to everlasting, Thou art God.
—Psalm 90:2

Everything and everyone has a beginning. Everyone, that is, but God. He has always been and will always be. He has no birthday to celebrate, for He was never born, never created. God has never *not* existed. True, Mary gave birth to the baby Jesus in a Bethlehem stable. But before this miraculous incarnation, Jesus existed in eternity with God the Father (see John 1:1–3).

That's hard for our finite minds to grasp, isn't it? We all have birthdays. We all live on this earth a finite number of days. Our friendships, families, and jobs all have a starting point. Everything around us—houses, cars, clothes, even food—came from something.

God didn't *come* from anything. He has always been.

> In the great expanse of eternity, which stretches behind Genesis 1:1, the universe was unborn and creation existed only in the mind of the great Creator. In His sovereign majesty God dwelt all alone. . . . There were then no angels to hymn God's praises, no creatures to occupy His notice, no rebels to be brought into subjection. The great God was all alone amid the [profound] silence of His own vast universe.[1]

The eternal God . . . completely self-sufficient . . . dependent on no one outside of Himself.

Yet He chose to create. What a wondrous thought! The God who had no beginning and no end chose to bring into being the earth and the heavens, time and space, height and depth. And He chose to give us a beginning so we could enjoy the world He crafted

---

1. Arthur W. Pink, *The Sovereignty of God* (1930; reprint, Grand Rapids, Mich.: Baker Book House, 1994), p. 28.

GENESIS

	Creation CHAPTERS 1–2	Fall CHAPTERS 3–5	Flood CHAPTERS 6–9	Nations CHAPTERS 10–11	Abraham CHAPTERS 12–25	Isaac CHAPTERS 26–27	Jacob CHAPTERS 28–36	Joseph CHAPTERS 37–50
Beginnings	Beginning of the human race				Beginning of the chosen race			
Result	Confusion and scattering				Bondage in Egypt			
History	Primeval history				Patriarchal history			
Chronology	Over 2,000 years				Approximately 300 years			
Emphasis	Four major events				Four important people			
Key Words and Phrases	"In the beginning" (1:1) "Generations" (5:1; 6:9; 10:1; 11:10; 11:27; 25:12; 25:19; 36:1; 37:2)							
Christ in Genesis	Pictured in the seed of the woman (3:15); Melchizedek, the high priest (14:18); the humiliation and exaltation of Joseph (chapters 37–50)							

10

and embrace the One who crafted it.

Genesis, then, is appropriately the first book of the Bible. Not only does it begin with God's act of Creation, it sets the stage for the unfolding story of His relationship with us.

A Book of Beginnings

Everything about the book of Genesis—its name, its relationship to the rest of Scripture, and its structure—seems to say, "If it exists today, it began right here in Genesis."

Name

Between 250 and 150 B.C., in the midst of the intertestamental period, seventy Jewish scholars in Alexandria, Egypt, translated the Hebrew Scriptures into Greek, the common language of the day. In this translation, called the Septuagint, they titled the first book of the Law *Genesis*, a Greek word meaning "origin, source, generation, or beginning." The name carried over to the English Bible. The original Hebrew title of the book is *Bereshith*, which means "In the Beginning."[2]

Relationship to the Rest of Scripture

The first five books of the Bible make up the Pentateuch (from *penta*, the Greek word for *five*, and *teuchos*, which means *tool*). Each of the five books were written by Moses, and fit together to provide some insight about humanity, God, and the difference between them.

Book of the Pentateuch	What It Tells Us about Humanity	What It Tells Us about God
Genesis	Ruin and rebellion through sin	Sovereignty
Exodus	Redemption from bondage	Omnipotence
Leviticus	Communion and fellowship	Holiness
Numbers	Redirection	Justice
Deuteronomy	Instruction	Faithfulness

2. Bruce Wilkinson and Kenneth Boa, *Talk Thru the Old Testament*, vol. 1 of *Talk Thru the Bible*, (Nashville, Tenn.: Thomas Nelson Publishers, 1983), p. 6.

Literary Structure

Genesis, then, is the book of beginnings. The beginning of time. The beginning of life and human fellowship with God. The beginning of sin and salvation, judgment and grace. The beginning of work and worship. The beginning of marriage and family. This theme recurs throughout the book as we read of beginnings and generations, which authors Bruce Wilkinson and Kenneth Boa list for us.

> (1) Introduction to the Generations (1:1–2:3); (2) Heaven and Earth (2:4–4:26); (3) Adam (5:1–6:8); (4) Noah (6:9–9:29); (5) Sons of Noah (10:1–11:9); (6) Shem (11:10–26); (7) Terah (11:27–25:11); (8) Ishmael (25:12–18); (9) Isaac (25:19–35:29); (10) Esau (36:1–37:1); (11) Jacob (37:2–50:26).[3]

Within this overarching theme, we find that, structurally, Genesis has two main sections: chapters 1–11, which primarily cover *events*; and chapters 12–50, which mainly focus on *people*. The following chart distinguishes these contrasts.

Genesis 1–11	Genesis 12–50
• Time: covers about 2000 years	• Time: covers about 300 years
• Emphasizes events:	• Emphasizes people:
1. Creation (chaps. 1–2)	1. Abraham (chaps. 12–25:18)[5]
2. Fall (chaps. 3–5)[4]	2. Isaac (chaps. 25:19–27)
3. Flood (chaps. 6–9)	3. Jacob (chaps. 28–36)
4. Nations (chaps. 10–11)	4. Joseph (chaps. 37–50)

Though the book of Genesis divides nicely into two main sections, don't mistake this division for disunity. The two sections

---

3. Wilkinson and Boa, *Talk Thru the Old Testament*, p. 6.

4. "In the first sin man is separated from God (Adam from God), and in the second sin, man is separated from man (Cain from Abel)." Wilkinson and Boa, *Talk Thru the Old Testament*, pp. 8–9.

5. "The calling of Abraham . . . is the pivotal point of the book. The three covenant promises God makes to Abraham (land, descendants, and blessing) are foundational to His program of bringing salvation upon the earth." Wilkinson and Boa, *Talk Thru the Old Testament*, p. 9.

are critically linked. The people of Abraham's line in chapters 12–50 grow out of the events in chapters 1–11. If there had never been a fall, which perpetuated wickedness in the world and drew God's judgment, there would have been no need for God to call and preserve Abraham's family to be His chosen family from whom the Messiah would come.

From Abraham's time forward, you see, God's focus is on His people whom He promised to bless and protect.[6] Simply put, the rest of the Old Testament is a record of God's dealings with His people, the Hebrews or Israelites, and His fulfillment of the promises stated in Genesis 12:1–3:

> Now the Lord said to Abram,
>   "Go forth from your country,
>   And from your relatives
>   And from your father's house,
>   To the land which I will show you;
>   And I will make you a great nation,
>   And I will bless you,
>   And make your name great;
>   And so you shall be a blessing;
>   And I will bless those who bless you,
>   And the one who curses you I will curse.
>   And in you all the families of the earth shall
>   be blessed."

That last promise came true because God preserved a messianic line through Abraham. His son Isaac had Esau and Jacob. Jacob had twelve sons; and it was through his fourth son, Judah, that Israel's kingly line and ultimate King, Jesus, would come.

Key Verse

All Scripture, including Abraham's story, unfolds from one seminal verse in Genesis 3. Author Anthony Hoekema explains:

> The narrative of the fall found in the opening verses
> of Genesis 3 is followed immediately by the promise
> of a future redeemer in verse 15: "I will put enmity

---

6. The rest of the "Literary Structure" section is adapted from Lee Hough, from the study guide *A Look at the Book*, coauthored by Lee Hough and Bryce Klabunde, from the Bible-teaching ministry of Charles R. Swindoll (Anaheim, Calif.: Insight for Living, 1994), p. 33.

between you and the woman, and between your seed and her seed; he shall bruise your head, and you shall bruise his heel." This passage, often called the "mother promise," now sets the tone for the entire Old Testament. The words are addressed to the serpent, later identified as an agent of Satan (Rev. 12:9; 20:2). The enmity placed between mankind and the serpent implies that God, who is also the serpent's enemy, will be man's friend. In the prediction that ultimately the seed of the woman will bruise the serpent's head we have the promise of the coming redeemer. We may say that in this passage God reveals, as in a nutshell, all of his saving purpose with his people. The further history of redemption will be an unfolding of the contents of this mother promise. From this point on, all of Old Testament revelation looks forward, points forward, and eagerly awaits the promised redeemer.[7]

This Redeemer is fully revealed in the New Testament as the Lord Jesus Christ. Genesis, then, sets the stage, not just for the progression of history, but for God's great program of delivering the human race from sin.

Application

The grand scope of Genesis, however, does not overshadow its personal significance. Consider how the book touches our lives as individual believers.

- *God created us.* He knit us together, crafted us in His own image. We are "fearfully and wonderfully made" (Ps. 139:14). Creation means that God took a personal interest in us before we knew anything about Him. And He created us for relationship with Himself.

- *God re-created us.* Adam rebelled against his Creator, and so have we all. Knowing that even the smallest of sins would keep us distant from Him, our holy God made a way to bring us close.

7. Anthony A. Hoekema, *The Bible and the Future* (Grand Rapids, Mich.: William B. Eerdmans Publishing Co., 1979), pp. 4–5.

When we put our faith in Christ, we stepped into His righteousness and were made anew (see 2 Cor. 5:17). As Noah and his family were kept safe from God's judgment inside the ark, we are safe from God's judgment in Christ . . . and welcomed into His loving care.

- *God is using us in His re-creation of others.* As new creations in Christ, we have the privilege of sharing His gospel with others. We're representatives of His kingdom, heralds of His message. We testify to the reality of His presence and the truth of His Word. If we didn't have a purpose in life before we knew Christ, we have one now.

Genesis. The beginning of all things—maybe even the start of a renewed love and appreciation for Him who made us.

Living Insights

Genesis 3:15, as Anthony Hoekema noted earlier, foreshadows the coming Redeemer, Jesus Christ. But what happens to Him between Genesis and the New Testament? Well, let's take a quick perusal through the Bible, and take note of where He appears.

In the Book of . . .	*He is . . .*
Genesis	The woman's Seed
Exodus	The Passover Lamb
Leviticus	The atoning Sacrifice
Numbers	The bronze Serpent
Deuteronomy	The promised Prophet
Joshua	The unseen Captain
Judges	My Deliverer
Ruth	My heavenly Kinsman
Samuel, Kings, Chronicles	The promised King
Ezra and Nehemiah	The Restorer of the nation
Esther	My Advocate
Job	My Redeemer
Psalms	My All in All

In the Book of . . .	*He is . . .*
Proverbs	My Pattern
Ecclesiastes	My Goal
Song of Solomon	My Beloved
The Prophets	The coming Prince of Peace
Matthew	Christ the King
Mark	Christ the Servant
Luke	Christ the Son of Man
John	Christ the Son of God
Acts	Risen, seated, and sending
The Epistles	Indwelling and filling
Revelation	Returning and reigning[8]

He's everywhere! Jesus Christ runs through the Scripture like a recurring melody. He is the theme of revelation, the tune of the ages, the everlasting song.

What does that tell you about how much God wants us to know His Son and the work He has done on our behalf?

_____

_____

_____

Since Christ is so thoroughly presented in Scripture, what would you say is the best way to get to know Him better?

_____

_____

_____

Are you taking in enough Scripture to grow close to Him? Are you approaching your reading and study with the goal of knowing Him more intimately?

8. Adapted from *Illustrating Great Words of the New Testament*, by J. B. Fowler, Jr. (Nashville, Tenn.: Broadman Press, 1991), p. 98.

_____

_____

_____

What has God revealed to you so far about His Son in this survey of Genesis?

_____

_____

_____

_____

_____

For a picture of someone who foreshadowed Christ, take a look at Jacob's son Joseph in Genesis 37, 39–45, 50. What resemblances do you see there?

_____

_____

_____

_____

Why not take some time right now to thank God for revealing His Son to you. Ask Him to guide you during the rest of this series, drawing you close to Christ.

Chapter 3

EXODUS: STORY OF MIRACULOUS FREEDOM

A *Survey of Exodus*

Every May, millions of Americans rummage through their closets, digging behind the umbrellas and golf clubs to find and unfurl Old Glory. Soon, wooden picnic tables are decked out in red-and-white-checked tablecloths. And swimming pools, lakes, and beaches draw humanity like a melted Popsicle draws ants. For one long weekend, it's hard to take a breath without picking up the scent of backyard barbecues, suntan lotion, or sizzling hot dogs.

It's Memorial Day, a time of fun and celebration. But it's also a time of solemn reflection.

Many families and friends plant a small flag near a loved one's gravestone, until the silent hillsides of the cemeteries are hallowed with remembrance of youth, courage, sacrifice, and loss. Tears blur the names etched into battle monuments and war memorials. And pastors, priests, and politicians uphold the memory of those who fought and died for freedom.

Yes, we relish our freedom, but it came at a great price. So enjoying and remembering go hand in hand. We are free because someone went before us to set us free.

Do you know the same is true with our spiritual lives? As Christians, we can enjoy peace with God. We're part of His family. Instead of being enslaved to our old master, sin, we're free to love and obey God and serve in His church.

But we wouldn't have that freedom if God had not gone before us to secure it. Long before Jesus came in the flesh, God put together a plan to redeem us through His Son. Had He not chosen to act on our behalf, we would never have known spiritual freedom. That's what the book of Exodus is all about—God's rescuing, sustaining, and preserving His people when they're unable to help themselves.

So let's unfurl the scroll of Exodus and let it serve as our flag of freedom. May it not only remind us of the gift of freedom but draw us closer to the God who gave it.

EXODUS

	Bondage	Deliverance	Journey	Law	Tabernacle
	Israelites became numerous New Pharaoh Plan to destroy Israelites Moses	Blood Frogs Gnats Flies Livestock — Boils Hail Locusts Darkness Death Passover Exodus	Cloud and fire Red Sea Grumbling	Moral Civil Social	Outer court 150' x 75' Inner court 45' x 15'
	CHAPTERS 1–2	*CHAPTERS 3–12*	*CHAPTERS 13–18*	*CHAPTERS 19–24*	*CHAPTERS 25–40*

Groan of the Israelites — 350 Years — GENESIS

Glory of the Lord

Place	Egypt		En route	Mount Sinai	
Time	430 years		3 months	1 year	
Theme	Suffering and liberation of people of God		Guidance of God	Worship of God	
Key Verses	6:6; 12:40–42; 19:5–6				
Christ in Exodus	Passover lamb (chap. 12): sacrificial offering, tabernacle, articles of worship (chaps. 25–40); His leadership and deliverance are pictured in Moses; His purity and intercession are pictured in the high priest				

19

The Name: Exodus

Exodus, like *Genesis*, comes to us from the Greek version of the Old Testament, the Septuagint. The word means "exit, departure, or going out," which describes the book's key event: the departure of the Hebrews from Egypt to become God's holy nation.

The Hebrew title of the book, *We'elleh Shemoth*, simply echoes the opening phrase, "And these are the names." The "and" in the Hebrew connects us with the end of the book of Genesis (see NASB margin note). So Exodus begins with the story of how Jacob's family, now in Egypt, began to grow and prosper.

A Survey of the Content

To get the flow of the story, let's recap the final few chapters of Genesis. Joseph, one of Jacob's sons, had been sold into slavery by his jealous brothers who told their father that he had been killed by wild beasts. Through an amazing chain of events orchestrated by God's sovereign hand, Joseph rose to power in Egypt, second in position only to Pharaoh himself.

Completely trusted by Pharaoh, Joseph was put in charge of grain distribution during a severe famine. His brothers, unaware of his position, came to Egypt to buy grain during the shortage. Joseph eventually revealed his identity and forgave his brothers. Pharaoh then welcomed Joseph's family into Egypt and provided them with land and a livelihood. And the Hebrews prospered.

> And all the persons who came from the loins of Jacob were seventy in number, but Joseph was already in Egypt. And Joseph died, and all his brothers and all that generation. But the sons of Israel were fruitful and increased greatly, and multiplied, and became exceedingly mighty, so that the land was filled with them. (Exod. 1:5–7)

So the future looked pretty bright for the Hebrews . . . or did it?

Chapters 1–2: Bondage

In the next verses, a dark shadow of doubt falls over the Hebrews' future as a new Pharaoh comes to power.

> Now a new king arose over Egypt, who did not know Joseph. And he said to his people, "Behold,

the people of the sons of Israel are more and mightier than we. Come, let us deal wisely with them, lest they multiply and in the event of war, they also join themselves to those who hate us, and fight against us, and depart from the land." (vv. 8–10)

Now there's an example of a man whose fears got the better of him! The king's insecurity rapidly turned into oppression, as he tried to subdue the descendants of Jacob. But the Hebrews continued to grow strong and numerous. Infanticide seemed to be the only answer, so Pharaoh ordered the Hebrew midwives to put to death every Hebrew male infant they helped deliver. The midwives, however, feared God more than they feared the king and preserved the boys' lives.

While these little boys were being delivered from death, God's plan for delivering the whole Hebrew race was coming together.

One Hebrew woman, afraid for her son's life, nestled the baby in a basket and hid him among some reeds in the Nile. Pharaoh's daughter discovered the boy and decided to keep him as her own. Ironically, she unknowingly hired his real mother to nurse him. So, nurtured on Hebrew milk, Hebrew blood pumping through his veins, Moses grew up in the courts of Egypt. He learned the customs, the language, the religion—seemingly being groomed for Egypt. But God had a greater plan.

Not aware of God's plan but still wanting to help his people, Moses took matters into his own hands and killed an Egyptian who was beating a Hebrew slave. Word spread quickly to Pharaoh, who sought to kill Moses. So Moses fled to the land of Midian and settled there as a shepherd . . . until God called him to lead a different kind of flock.

Chapters 3–12: Deliverance

Forty years in Egypt. Forty more years in the desert of Midian. Moses was now eighty years old. At the age most men are ready to hang it up, God called Moses to the greatest challenge of his life—the deliverance of the Hebrew people.

> [God's] grand plan centered around a certain broken-down, eighty-year-old shepherd in the wastes of Sinai. Moses was a long way from the refined gentleman he had been. Wind-burned and sun-darkened, his beard long and his hair wild, he

21

was typecast to play the desert prophet marching into the Egyptian court. . . .

One dusty day in the shadow of Mount Sinai, the shepherd caught sight of a bush on fire but not being consumed. As he drew near, a voice from within the flames called his name. "Do not come any closer," said the voice. "Take off your sandals, for the place where you are standing is holy ground. I am the God of your father, the God of Abraham, the God of Isaac, and the God of Jacob." Moses was terrified.

"I have indeed seen the misery of My people in Egypt," God went on. "So I have come down to rescue them. So I am sending you to Pharaoh to bring My people the Israelites out of Egypt."[1]

Moses resisted the commission and tried to convince God that he was unqualified for the task. But God responded that the power for deliverance rested with Himself. He had determined to free His people from bondage, so the plan was set. Moses and his brother Aaron went back to Egypt to confront Pharaoh.

Pharaoh, of course, wasn't about to release his huge Hebrew labor force. He resisted Moses' repeated demands to free the Israelites until, finally, after seeing the power of God displayed in a series of ten plagues, he had no choice but to let the people go.

During the final plague—the death of Egypt's first-born—God demonstrated His special love for and protection of Israel with the institution of the Passover. "Passed over" by the Lord because of the sacrificial lamb's blood on their doorposts, the Hebrews now knew they were God's possession.

> And it came about at the end of four hundred and thirty years, to the very day, that all the hosts of the Lord went out from the land of Egypt. (Exod. 12:41)

Chapters 13–18: Journey

So out of Egypt the Hebrews followed their deliverer, Moses, who was in turn led by God, the ultimate Deliverer. They were to be His people, and He was to be their God. They were to worship

---

1. Karen Lee-Thorp, *The Story of Stories*, rev. ed. (Colorado Springs, Colo.: NavPress, 1995), pp. 39–40.

Him and remember His protection by celebrating the Passover. And He would escort them—by cloud and fire—to the land He had promised Abraham centuries before. It didn't take long, though, for the people to start wondering if Moses, and God, knew what they were doing.

The Israelites, all two million of them, suddenly found themselves pinned against the sea with Pharaoh's army fast approaching. Pharaoh, having realized the huge economic and social hole the Hebrews' absence would leave in his kingdom, was on his way to bring them back by force.

Panic-stricken, the Hebrews turned on Moses. "Is it because there were no graves in Egypt that you have taken us away to die in the wilderness?" they grumbled (Exod. 14:11). But God hadn't brought them out to die. He had brought them out to be witnesses of His great power. He made a pathway through the Red Sea, and after the Israelites crossed over, God brought the waters crashing down on the pursuing Egyptian army.

In rescuing them and destroying their enemies, God showed His people that He was not only the God who frees, but the God who stays close for the whole journey. Through all their grumbling and lack of faith, God miraculously provided water for them to drink and bread for them to eat.[2] Finally, they came to Sinai, where God was ready to give them His law.

Chapters 19–24: Law

The plan of deliverance had now come full circle, with God bringing the Israelites to the very mountain where He had earlier commissioned Moses. Now it was the people who would be commissioned—to obey God, follow His laws, and be a holy nation.

The Mosaic Law includes not only the Ten Commandments, which serve as a summary of God's moral standards (Exod. 20), but all the civil and social instructions to God's people as well (chaps. 21–23). Having heard God's law, the Israelites enthusiastically agreed to live by it (24:7).

They soon discovered, however, what God already knew—sinful people can't obey the law of God in their own strength.

---

2. Both the water from the rock and the manna are symbols for the presence of Christ with His people and His endless supply of spiritual nourishment (see John 4:10–14; 6:31–35; 1 Cor. 10:1–4).

This brings up an interesting question. Our propensity is to sin. So why did God give the law if He knew we couldn't keep it? First, the law illustrates God's character. God is holy, good, pure, righteous. We, however, are not, which the law reveals quite clearly. We must obtain holiness, goodness, purity, and righteousness from an outside source . . . from God Himself. So a second purpose of the law is to make us aware of our own sinfulness and drive us to Christ, from whom we receive cleansing from sin and right standing before God (see Rom. 7:7; Gal. 3:24).

Chapters 25–40: Tabernacle

The remainder of the book of Exodus is dedicated to the construction and operation of the tabernacle, the place God designated for sacrifice and worship during the Israelites' nomadic days. The largest section of the book, these sixteen chapters provide God's detailed instructions about the tabernacle—its dimensions, materials, maintenance, and purity.

Why such an emphasis on building a tent in the desert? What do rams' skins, wooden poles, and sacrifices have to do with the spiritual life? Pastor and author James Montgomery Boice explains the ultimate lesson of the tabernacle.

> We have a dramatization of the holiness of God in the laws given for the building of the Jewish tabernacle. On one level, the tabernacle was constructed to teach the immanence of God, the truth that God is always present with his people. But on the other hand, it also taught that God is separated from his people because of his holiness and their sin, and can therefore be approached only in the way he determines. . . . The point of the tabernacle was that a sinful man or woman could not simply "barge in" upon the Holy One. God was understood to have dwelt symbolically within the innermost chamber of the tabernacle, known as the "Holy of Holies." . . . Only one person could ever go in; that was the high priest of Israel; and even he could go in only once a year and that only after having first made sacrifices for himself and the people in the outer courtyard.[3]

3. James Montgomery Boice, *Foundations of the Christian Faith*, rev. ed. (Downers Grove, Ill.: InterVarsity Press, 1986), pp. 128–29.

The writer of Hebrews revealed later in the New Testament that the tabernacle worship symbolized Christ:

> But when Christ appeared as a high priest of the good things to come, He entered through the greater and more perfect tabernacle, not made with hands, that is to say, not of this creation; and not through the blood of goats and calves, but through His own blood, He entered the holy place once for all, having obtained eternal redemption. For if the blood of goats and bulls and the ashes of a heifer sprinkling those who have been defiled, sanctify for the cleansing of the flesh, how much more will the blood of Christ, who through the eternal Spirit offered Himself without blemish to God, cleanse your conscience from dead works to serve the living God? (Heb. 9:11–14; see also 8:1–6)

By sacrificing His own Son, who bore our sins on His body when He hung on the cross, God through Jesus has given access to the Holy One. Jesus is our High Priest, clean and pure. Look closely at the closing chapters of Exodus, and you'll see more than blueprints for a tent. You'll see the nail prints of a Savior.

Internalizing Exodus

Three personal applications stand out from this book.

First, *lasting freedom is a direct result of God's intervention.* As good as national freedom is, it's only temporal. Spiritual freedom, however, begins here and lasts forever. When God pulls us out of sin's grip, He sets us free forever. We belong to Him, and we'll be with Him throughout eternity.

Second, *when God brings deliverance, He uses choice instruments in the process.* Moses was a deliverer. And Christ, of course, is the ultimate bringer of freedom. But others become deliverers, in a sense, when they tell us about the freedom we have in Christ. God may even want to use you to saw off the shackles of someone's captivity with the good news of Jesus Christ.

Third, *freedom must be balanced with submission to God's authority.* The Israelites, though miraculously delivered from Egypt, continued to disobey and complain against God. That's not why the Lord frees us, though. He wants us to walk *toward* Him, not away from Him.

In Christ, we have the ability to obey. We're free to follow. That, in a nutshell, is the message of Exodus.

 ## Living Insights

Freedom isn't always easy. It's often unpredictable and sometimes dangerous. In fact, freedom can get downright scary. Just ask the Israelites. Freedom got so tough for them that they wanted to go back to Egypt: "It would have been better for us to serve the Egyptians than to die in the wilderness" (Exod. 14:12b). And this was after God afflicted Egypt with ten plagues and led the Israelites out of there with the nation's wealth in their pockets.

They grumbled again after walking through the Red Sea. And again after God provided manna. And again after he brought water from a rock.

Why is it that present hardship so often causes us to forget God's past faithfulness? Maybe we need to live in the past a little more, remembering how God has shown Himself trustworthy on our spiritual journey.

Have you done that lately? Why not make a list of things God has done for you this week, this month, this past year. Securing a new job. Keeping you in an old one. Comforting your family during a tragedy. Keeping you from harm. Gently teaching you about His love and mercy. Leading you to new friends.

_____

_____

_____

_____

_____

_____

_____

_____

Now, keep this list handy for the next memory lapse.

Chapter 4

LEVITICUS: GOD'S PICTURE BOOK ON WORSHIP
A Survey of Leviticus

Imagine you're spending an evening at the symphony. The orchestra is in the middle of a soothing presentation of Antonio Vivaldi's *The Four Seasons*. Suddenly the music stops. The conductor faces the audience and begins explaining the technical aspects of the composition. "Notice how the fermata punctuated that last measure," he says proudly. "Were you moved to tears by that dotted eighth rest?"

You want to cry, all right—not because you care about a dotted eighth rest, but because you're sad the music stopped.

Leviticus often has this same effect on many readers. The narrative flow of Genesis and Exodus seems harshly interrupted by the ceremonial and sacrificial details of this book. Anxious for the music to continue, many readers either rush through Leviticus or bypass it altogether.

But just as the underlying technical elements of a musical composition are essential to its overall performance, so Leviticus is crucial to the symphony of Scripture. It may strike us as cumbersome or unnecessary at first, but the more we listen to it, the more we'll come to appreciate its beauty and perfect placement in God's revelation. The editors of the *New Geneva Study Bible* expressed the importance of Leviticus this way:

> It is important to try to understand the rituals in Leviticus for two reasons. First, rituals enshrine, express, and teach those values and ideas that a society holds most dear. By analyzing the ceremonies described in Leviticus, we can learn about what was most important to the Old Testament Israelites. Second, these same ideas are foundational for the New Testament writers. Particularly the concepts of sin, sacrifice, and atonement found in Leviticus are used in the New Testament to interpret the death of Christ.
>
> . . . Leviticus speaks to humanity in every age, reminding us of the depth of our sin, but also pointing

LEVITICUS

	The Way to God *Access*	The Walk with God *Lifestyle*
	The approach: Offerings	Practical guidelines
	The representative: Priest	Chronological observances
	The laws: Cleansing *Physically* *Spiritually*	Severe consequences Verbal promises
	CHAPTERS 1–17	*CHAPTERS 18–27*
Emphasis	Ritual (for worship)	Practical (for living)
Location	Mount Sinai . . . one full year	
Key Question	How can sinful humanity worship a holy God?	
Key Verses	17:11; 19:2; 20:7–8	
Key Term	"Holy" (occurs 90 times)	
Christ in Leviticus	Pictured in each sacrifice and ritual	

us to the sacrifice of Him whose blood is far more effective than the blood of bulls and goats.[1]

With that in mind, let's take a look at this book and its pencil portraits of Christ.

A Bit of Background

A little history will help us understand the contents of Leviticus.

The Name

Leviticus, the Latin form of the Greek title of the book, means "about Levites" or "pertaining to the Levites."

> The Levites were the tribe of Israel from which the priests were drawn; they were responsible for maintaining Israel's worship facilities and practices. The title is apt, because the book is primarily about worship and fitness for worship. However it is not addressed solely to priests or Levites, but also to lay Israelites, telling them how to offer sacrifices and to enter the presence of God in worship.[2]

The Occasion

Why was Leviticus written, and what purpose did it serve in the life of the Israelites? The book of Exodus, remember, chronicles the deliverance of the Hebrew people. God delivered them *from* Egypt *to* Himself in order to make them a holy nation, God's own possession (see Exod. 19:5–6). Leviticus details *how* the Israelites were to become a holy nation—how they were to revere God and approach His presence, how they were to treat one another, and how they were to reflect God in every area of life.

The content of Leviticus was given to the Israelites during the year they camped at the foot of Mount Sinai. This was after they left Egypt and before they began their wilderness wanderings. Commentator R. Laird Harris explains that, during that year,

> Moses spent eighty days on the mountain with God.

---

1. *New Geneva Study Bible*, gen. ed. R. C. Sproul, Old Testament ed. Bruce Waltke (Nashville, Tenn.: Thomas Nelson Publishers, 1995), pp. 153, 154.

2. *New Geneva Study Bible*, p. 154.

Then the people of Israel, at Moses' instruction, built the wilderness tabernacle. During this year Moses organized the nation, built up the army, established courts and laws, and ordered formal worship. It was a busy year. Although most of the laws . . . that Moses drew up at that time are found in Exodus and Numbers, Leviticus is the law book *par excellence*.[3]

While camped at the foot of God's mountain, the Israelites learned that God was interested in more than just rescuing them. He wanted a relationship with them. He was willing to come down from His mountain to dwell among them and bridge the gap between deity and humanity.

A Survey of the Structure

Leviticus falls neatly into two main sections: The way to God (chapters 1–17) and the walk with God (chapters 18–27).

The Way to God: Chapters 1–17

Laws concerning offerings: Chapters 1–7. In His mercy, God provided a way for sinful humanity to approach their holy God— through a blood sacrifice, the innocent dying vicariously for the guilty. This is summed up in Leviticus' key verse:

> "'For the life of the flesh is in the blood, and I have given it to you on the altar to make atonement for your souls; for it is the blood by reason of the life that makes atonement.'" (17:11; see also Heb. 9:22)

That sounds strange, even barbaric, to us sophisticated twentieth-century folk. But that's the plan God put together. Leviticus reminds us that if we're to receive forgiveness and cleansing we must come to God on His terms.

The first seven chapters of Leviticus prescribe the proper manner for the Hebrew laity and priesthood to offer sacrifices to the Lord. The five types of offerings all depict a different characteristic of Jesus Christ, the ultimate sacrifice.

---

3. R. Laird Harris, "Leviticus," in *The Expositor's Bible Commentary* (Grand Rapids, Mich.: Zondervan Publishing House, Academic and Professional Books, 1990), pp. 501–2.

Levitical Offering	Picture of Christ
Burnt Offering (chap. 1; 6:8–13)	His total consecration to His Father's will
Grain Offering (chap. 2; 6:14–23)	His sinless service
Peace Offering (chap. 3; 7:11–36)	His work on the cross, which enables us to fellowship with God
Sin Offering (4:1–5:13; 6:24–30)	His bearing of our sins
Guilt Offering (5:14–6:7; 7:1–10)	His payment for the damage of sin

Laws concerning the priesthood: Chapters 8–10. This section describes all the specifics of priestly duty, including what to wear, how to prepare, which animals to sacrifice and how to offer them, where to stand, what to say, what to drink, and what to eat. Talk about an intimidating job description! Chapter 10 shows us what happened when these laws were taken lightly by two of Aaron's sons. God has never taken worship lightly. And neither should we.

Laws for purity: Chapters 11–17. Adding to the picture of the distance between a holy God and sinful humanity, chapters 11–17 emphasize cleanness and uncleanness in diet, hygiene, disease, and the Day of Atonement.

The Walk with God: Chapters 18–27

Having laid out the specifics for approaching God in chapters 1–17, Moses next details the requirements for walking with God on a daily basis.

Holy living: Chapters 18–22. It only makes sense that a God who allows us to approach Him would expect us to follow Him. He told the Israelites,

> "'You shall not do what is done in the land of Egypt where you lived, nor are you to do what is done in the land of Canaan where I am bringing you; you shall not walk in their statutes. You are to perform My judgments and keep My statutes, to live in accord with them; I am the Lord your God. So you shall keep My statutes and My judgments, by which a man may live if he does them; I am the Lord.'" (18:3–5)

Since the Israelites belonged to a holy God, they were expected to be holy themselves (19:2; 20:7). Every area of life—family relationships, worship, sexuality, the treatment of the poor, even personal grooming—were to reflect the purity of God's character.

Holy times: Chapters 23–25. The next three chapters focus on the festivals the Israelites were to celebrate. *Harper's Bible Dictionary* tells us these

> feasts and festivals were occasions of joy. They were times for thanking God for blessings and granting relief to the poor and oppressed. They were often accompanied by singing, instrumental music, dancing, elaborate meals, and sacrifices.[4]

Also, the festivals, just like the tabernacle and sacrifices, pictured the Messiah who was to come.

> Passover speaks of the substitutionary death of the Lamb of God. Christ died on the day of Passover. Unleavened Bread speaks of the holy walk of the believer (1 Cor. 5:6–8). Firstfruits speaks of Christ's resurrection as the firstfruit of the resurrection of all believers (1 Cor. 15:20–23). Christ rose on the day of the Firstfruits. Pentecost speaks of the descent of the Holy Spirit after Christ's ascension. Trumpets, the Day of Atonement, and Tabernacles speak of events associated with the second advent of Christ. This may be why these three are separated by a long gap from the first four in Israel's annual cycle.[5]

So the festivals serve not only to remind the Israelites of their relationship to God but also to sketch out a picture of the person and work of Jesus Christ.

In chapter 26, God warns Israel that He will prosper them if they obey his commands . . . and judge them if they don't. Chapter 27 closes the book with guidelines for dedicating people, animals, and possessions to the Lord.

---

4. Paul J. Achtemier *Harper's Bible Dictionary* on Logos Software (San Francisco, Calif.: Harper and Row, Publishers, 1985).

5. Bruce Wilkinson and Kenneth Boa, *Talk Thru the Bible* (Nashville, Tenn.: Thomas Nelson Publishers, 1983), p. 22. Though the Day of Atonement clearly represents the "once for all" sacrifice of Christ for sin, its grouping with the Day of Trumpets and Day of Tabernacles may also suggest the salvation of the Jews at Jesus' second coming.

Leviticus for Today

How does this book of law apply to Christians today? We no longer lug lambs to the altar for sacrifice. Nor are our schedules stuffed with a regimen of ceremonial cleansing. And as far as festivals go, you'll find Christmas and Easter on a Christian calendar, but not the Feast of Tabernacles.

The book of Hebrews is our key to unlocking the spiritual significance of Leviticus. In fact, G. Campbell Morgan goes so far as to say:

> Leviticus and Hebrews are always to be kept together in your Bible study. I say frankly, to anyone who thinks he is studying Hebrews, if he does not study Leviticus also he does not know Hebrews, for one must know the Book of Leviticus to understand Hebrews. Hebrews shows a fulfilling of everything suggested in Leviticus.[6]

And for his part, the author of Hebrews tells us how those no longer under the Law should view the material in Leviticus: as symbols (Heb. 9:9), copies of heavenly realities (v. 23), "a shadow of the good things to come" (10:1). For what the Old Testament rituals pictured in type and shadow, Christ has performed in reality.

So when we read Leviticus, we should rejoice. Not only because we're free from the encumbering observance of ceremony and ritual, but because of the *reason* that we're free: Jesus Christ himself. We have no need to bring sacrifices, for He is the ultimate sacrifice. Daily priestly duties are no longer necessary, for He is the Great High Priest whose completed work on the cross gives us unhindered access to God. Through Christ we are cleansed. And only in Him can we fulfill God's command, "'You shall be holy, for I the Lord your God am holy'" (Lev. 19:2).

 Living Insights

For a Jew camped at the base of Sinai, learning about God wasn't an option. Every direction an Israelite turned, God was there.

---

6. G. Campbell Morgan, *The Unfolding Message of the Bible* (Westwood, N.J.: Fleming H. Revell Co., 1961), p. 51.

His holiness was represented by the veils in the tabernacle that separated Him from the camp. The treatment of diseases pictured God's disdain for sin and passion for purity. The bleating of sheep and the smell of burning carcasses served as a reminder of His gracious plan for bringing sinful humanity and holy deity together. The reality of the living God seeped into every niche of life.

Quite a different picture from the compartmentalized Christianity so prevalent today. God is often an add-on, just one more token in the game of life, one more slot on the schedule. He's real during Sunday worship, but He doesn't always permeate the rest of our lives.

Is God compartmentalized in your life, or does He fill every niche? Is He an add-on, or is He everything?

_____

_____

_____

_____

In which areas of your life does He seem to be left out?

_____

_____

_____

Take some time to pray and ask God to fill those niches. This week, give special attention to those "compartments," bringing down those walls and letting Him in.

 *Digging Deeper*

So much in Exodus and Leviticus foreshadows Christ—it's a fascinating study. But more than that, when you know what the substance behind the shadow is, the Scriptures burst with new meaning and life. The following chart shows some of the key Old Testament shadows with their New Testament realities.

Shadow	Substance
tabernacle	gospel
sanctuary (Holy Place and Holy of Holies)	heaven
outer court	earth
tabernacle furniture	ministries of Christ
brazen altar	Calvary
laver	Christ's sinlessness
candlestick	ministry of imparting the Holy Spirit
table of shewbread	sustaining power of Christ for the believer
incense altar	Christ's ministry of intercession
Holy of Holies	presence of God
ark of the covenant	God's justice
mercy seat	God's mercy
veil	access to God granted through Christ's physical death
high priest	Christ
Levites	ministers of the Gospel
physical perfection of priest, sacrificial animals	Christ's sinlessness
blood	Christ's life and sacrificial death
scapegoat	Christ's death outside the gates of Jerusalem
Day of Atonement	Christ's one sacrifice for the sins of the world

Shadow	Substance
animal sacrifices	Christ's life and sacrificial death
burnt offerings	consecration of Christ to God, consecration of saints to God
grain offering	service of Christ to humanity, our service to one another
sin offering	Christ's provision of atonement, our appropriation of it
peace offering	our reconciliation to God through Christ's sacrifice, reconciliation with each other
Egypt	the world and its bondage
Canaan	the world of the believer's freedom and victory in God
Israel	the church, God's people
wilderness	backslidden believers[7]

7. Adapted from Roy Lee DeWitt, *Teaching from the Tabernacle* (1986; reprint, Grand Rapids, Mich.: Baker Book House, 1988), p. 103.

Chapter 5

NUMBERS: A TRAGIC PILGRIMAGE

A Survey of Numbers

As Judah stood before this innocent man hanging on a cross, he probably didn't realize that he was standing right where God wanted him. His journey, like that of the crucified man, had reached its predetermined destination.

Once a prominent Jew, wealthy and well-respected in the community, Judah lost everything in a flash of confusion and betrayal. Convicted of a crime he didn't commit, he was sentenced to man the oars of a Roman battleship, and his family was imprisoned.

God was still with Judah, though. On the way to the ship, he and his fellow slaves were marched through Nazareth. Faint from thirst and exhaustion, he received a drink from a carpenter whose compassion gave him the will to live. Later, he survived a bloody sea battle and saved a prominent Roman officer, who adopted him. By now an embittered, angry man, Judah used his new position and citizenship to confront his accuser and one-time friend, Messala.

In a deadly chariot race, Judah defeated Messala, who confessed that his family was still alive—but they had become lepers in prison. Judah heard about a man from Galilee who was healing the sick in Jerusalem, so he took his mother and sister there to find the healer. When they found Jesus, however, He was carrying a cross to Golgotha. Recognizing Him as the man who had given him water, Judah followed Jesus. And here again their paths converged.

As he watched the Son of God, he saw the unforgettable—and the unbelievable. He saw Jesus look down at His tormentors and ask the God of heaven to "forgive them, for they know not what they do." All the hatred Judah had clenched in his fists for the injustices in his life seemed to slip out of now open hands. At last, at the foot of the cross, Judah Ben-Hur found peace and forgiveness.

His was a hard journey, but a necessary one. Because it was God's plan to bring Judah Ben-Hur to the Cross . . . and to the Savior who died there.

If the movie *Ben Hur* has a lesson for Christians, it's that we're not alone on our spiritual journey. God is faithful, even when we're

NUMBERS

	Preparation	Pessimism	Punishment
	Census Organization Sanctification	Complaining Doubting Promised Land Rejected	Wandering Old Generation Dies New Census
	CHAPTERS 1–9	*CHAPTERS 10–14*	*CHAPTERS 15–36*
Time	20 Days	Several Months	38 Years
Place	Mount Sinai	En Route to Kadesh-Barnea	Wilderness Wandering
Theme	The price of disbelief and disobedience		
Key Verses		14:22–23	
Key Word		Wilderness	
Christ in Numbers	Pictured in manna (compare John 6:31–33); water from rock (compare 1 Cor. 10:4); bronze serpent (compare John 3:14); in Balaam's prophecy (Num. 24:17); pillar of cloud and of fire; cities of refuge		

not. He always knows where we're heading, even when we feel lost. He never abandons us, although we sometimes think He has. And His way is always best.

If only the Israelites had learned these lessons, the book of Numbers might read differently.

Preparing for the Promised Land

The Israelites had spent a year at the base of Mount Sinai receiving God's Law and building His tabernacle. Now, in preparation for their journey to the Promised Land, God ordered Moses to organize and number the people. The Septuagint picked up on this theme of numbering and gave the book the name Numbers. The Hebrew title, however, *Bemidbar*, emphasizes the wilderness wandering and means "in the wilderness."[1]

Can you imagine the logistics of moving an entire nation to another country? The census revealed a total of 603,550 men (Num. 2:32). And these were just the war-worthy men. This figure didn't include women, children, or Levites. So the complete company of Israelites could have easily numbered two and a half million or more. They had to pack up, dismantle the tabernacle, move, then set up camp somewhere else. And they did this time and time again.

Without getting too hung up on math, there's one more number worth noting. Toward the end of the book, God instructs Moses to take *another* census (26:2). It's almost forty years later, yet the total this time is 1,820 *fewer* men. What happened? The events that transpired between this second census and the first one tell us of God's faithfulness, and the consequences of His people's faithlessness.

A Panoramic View of the Journey

A panoramic view of Numbers will give us a sweeping survey of the book and a feel for how the wilderness wanderings fit into it. Three main sections chronicle the pilgrimage of the Israelites.

Mount Sinai: Chapters 1:1–10:10

What a time of anticipation this must have been for the Israelites! Delivered from slavery in Egypt. Recipients of God's holy Law. Objects of His faithful affection. Their identity would no

1. Bruce Wilkinson and Kenneth Boa, *Talk Thru the Old Testament*, vol. 1 of *Talk Thru the Bible* (Nashville, Tenn.: Thomas Nelson Publishers, 1983), p. 28.

longer depend on the nations around them. They were now the unique and personal possession of the Lord of heaven.

And God longed to fashion them into a holy nation that reflected His character (no small task). So He kept them at the foot of Mount Sinai for about one year—teaching them, organizing them, and preparing them to live in the land He had promised Abraham. This first section represents the final three weeks of the Israelites' encampment at Sinai.

The Road to Kadesh-Barnea: Chapters 10:11–14:45

After a year at Sinai, it was time to move. Picture the scene. The cloud of God rose above the tent of meeting and began to creep northward. Tent pegs came up, the Levites packed the tabernacle for transport, and the twelve tribes moved out in sequence. This was it! Like travelers on a long layover, the Israelites were finally cleared to leave Sinai and head toward the Promised Land.

But delight soon turned to discouragement as the Israelites began to grumble against God—which they tended to do when the journey got difficult. What did they complain about? The menu; they were tired of manna. Never mind that manna was God's miraculous, daily provision for them. Never mind that it kept them alive in the desert, where there were no fish or animals and few edible plants growing. And who cared that it was delivered to their camp fresh every morning (except on the Sabbath, when they had to gather a double portion the day before).

They wanted meat, like they had in Egypt. "You want meat?" God responded. "I'll give you meat." The sky grew black with quail, until the Israelites were knee-deep in the birds. As they were stuffing themselves, God's anger burned against them. As judgment for their grumbling, He struck them with a plague.

Interesting, isn't it. God sometimes gives us what we think we want, yet it doesn't satisfy if it's gained by distrust and disobedience.

It gets worse. Miriam and Aaron, Moses' own sister and brother, complained about Moses' leadership, which prompted God to strike Miriam with leprosy. The most amazing act of rebellion, though, and the turning point of the book, comes in chapter 13. At Kadesh-Barnea, the Israelites stood on the edge of the Promised Land. God sent twelve spies to check out the land—which He had already promised to give them—and all but two brought back a negative report. Soon the whole camp was filled with fear . . . and void of faith, except for Caleb, Joshua, and Moses.

That was the last straw. God had heard enough of their faithless complaining. He had no choice but to judge them. So He sentenced the Israelites to wander in the wilderness for thirty-eight years, allowing the generation of complainers to die off.

Wilderness Wanderings: Chapters 15–36

How sad. The generation of the Exodus would not be the generation of the conquest. Rather than taking this generation of complainers into His Promised Land, God decided to start over. Every man twenty years or older, except for Caleb, Joshua, and Moses, would die in the wilderness.

Despite this tragic judgment, the people continued to struggle with their stubbornness and disbelief. Korah led a rebellion against Moses, and the earth opened up and swallowed him and his followers alive in judgment. Still the Israelites grumbled against Moses and Aaron. So God had Moses gather twelve staffs from each of the tribes; then He miraculously made Aaron's staff bloom and bear almonds as irrefutable proof that he was God's choice.

Did that finally convince the people to respect Moses and Aaron, God's appointed leaders? Not when they were thirsty. This episode frustrated Moses so much that when God told him to *speak* to the rock and it would pour forth water (another shadow of Christ, by the way), he struck it twice instead. His disobedience cost even Moses the privilege of entering the Promised Land.

After thirty-eight years of grumbling and judgment, sinning and punishment, repenting and forgiveness, warring and deliverance, the new generation prepared to take possession of Canaan. They received new instructions, a new census was taken, and Joshua was named Moses' successor. Unlike their predecessors, this generation seemed to be listening to God and trusting in His protection.

Lessons from Numbers

The journeyings of the Israelites drive home three important truths.

1. *Complaining is usually contagious.* Complaining seldom stops with one person. The negative report from the spies at Kadesh-Barnea immediately got the rest of the camp grumbling. Through this episode and others, attitudes of ingratitude, self-absorption, fear, and desperation soon infiltrated the Israelites' ranks. So focused on themselves, they forgot God's goodness and their purpose as His

holy people. Let's remember that a positive trust in God can be equally infectious . . . and create much better results.

2. *Doubting is often disastrous.* There's a healthy kind of doubting, where we struggle with who God is and He reveals Himself to us in a way that strengthens our faith. Then there's the kind of doubting that's closer to downright disbelief.

The Israelites had seen God's power, faithfulness, provision, presence, and leadership. Yet they doubted His goodness and feared that He would not continue to protect them. They even thought God had brought them into the wilderness to destroy them! For their disbelief, they were judged. How often must God rescue us, feed us, protect us, and guide us before we're convinced of His faithfulness?

3. *Wandering is always humbling.* The Israelites were so close! When they refused to trust the Lord at Kadesh-Barnea, they were on the very outskirts of the Promised Land. They could have entered it in a matter of days. But God didn't want to covenant with a complaining, faithless people. So He made them wander around in the desert for thirty-eight years, until the old generation died off. Wandering, though it seems aimless, has a purpose if directed by God. He uses it to break our pride, humble our hearts, and start afresh.

 Living Insights

I don't own a camel. I only pitch a tent when I go camping (which is almost never). And I worship God in a church building, not a tabernacle. Yet I often feel a kinship with those ancient, nomadic Israelites. How often my spiritual journey mirrors their pilgrimage.

Sometimes I feel as though I'm sitting at the base of Sinai, marveling at God's holiness and soaking in His Word. During those times, I'm content to stay put and hear from Him. Other times, I seem to be perched on the edge of the Promised Land, eager to push ahead and take possession of all God has promised me. Then there are those wandering times, when I seem to take the long way, the hard way to God—the trip lengthened by my disobedience or desire for something besides God.

You've probably traveled a similarly diverse path. Those wandering times can cause us to meander into some real discouragement, can't they? The book of Numbers, though, has some good news for us: God has signed on for the whole trip. He doesn't abandon us just because we wander. He's with us in the wandering—guiding, prompting, disciplining, sustaining, forgiving, and renewing us. What seems like aimless wandering to us has purpose and direction if God is in it.

Where are you in your spiritual journey? Sitting under Sinai? Poised at the Promised Land? Or wandering in the wilderness?

_____

_____

Do you sense that God is with you on the journey?

_____

_____

If you're wondering where He is, the following passages just might be an encouragement to you. What evidence do you have of His presence? Take some time to read them; then write down what they say about God's faithfulness in the spiritual journey.

Deuteronomy 31:6 _____

_____

_____

Psalm 139:7–12 _____

_____

_____

Ephesians 1:3–14 _____

_____

_____

While you're wandering, there's no need to wonder. He's right there. And He always will be.

Chapter 6

DEUTERONOMY: REMEMBER! REMEMBER!

A Survey of Deuteronomy

Memory is a funny thing.

Consider, for example, the story of the three absent-minded sisters—Anabelle, Mabel, and Gladys—who all lived in the same house. One evening after chatting with her sisters, Anabelle announced she was going upstairs to take a bubble bath and go to bed. She filled the tub, eased one leg into the water . . . and stopped. "I can't remember," she said. "Was I getting in or out?" Unable to continue, she called her sister for help: "Mabel, can you come up here?"

"Coming, dear," said Mabel. She started up the stairs, making it to the landing . . . and stopped. "I can't remember," she said. "Was I going up or down?" Now it was Mabel's turn to call for help: "Gladys, can you help me?"

Gladys, shaking her head, lamented, "Those two sisters of mine. If they didn't have me to help them remember, they wouldn't make it through the day. I'm glad I'm not like that, knock on wood." She rapped twice on the coffee table, then said pleasantly in the direction of the front door, "Come in."

We all forget, don't we? Memory loss often amounts to little more than a mental hiccup in our daily routine. Sometimes, though, it can paralyze us and keep us from moving ahead. To get where we need to go, we need to remember where we've been.

That's why the Israelites needed the book of Deuteronomy; it reminded them of their past and prepared them for their future. The new generation of desert wanderers was about to enter the Promised Land. But before they could move ahead, they needed to recall and emblazon on their minds and hearts the precious heritage God had given them. As they reflected on God's faithfulness, they would build faith for the future.

Some Important Facts

A little background information will help us get a handle on this significant book.

DEUTERONOMY

WILDERNESS WANDERING | | | CONQUERING CANAAN

	Looking Back	Looking Up	Looking Ahead
	REMEMBER!	REMEMBER!	REMEMBER!
	Failure at Kadesh-Barnea	Blessings accompany obedience	The land is yours, possess it!
	Faithfulness of God	Compromises weaken distinctives	The Lord is holy, obey Him!
		Consequences follow disobedience	
	CHAPTERS 1–4	CHAPTERS 5–26	CHAPTERS 27–34
Location	Everything occurs on the edge of the Promised Land of Canaan		
Leadership	At the beginning of the book MOSES is the leader (34:5) . . .		. . . by the end of the book JOSHUA is the leader (1:38; 34:9)
Time	The sermons recorded in Deuteronomy were first spoken (1:6) then written (31:24) during a period of forty days; (compare Deuteronomy 1:3; 34:8; and Joshua 4:19)		
Key Verses	6:4–9; 10:12–13; 30:19–20		
Key Message	Remember to love the Lord your God and keep His commandments		
Christ in Deuteronomy	"The Lord your God will 'raise up for you a prophet like me from among you, from your countrymen, you shall listen to him" (18:15); Moses himself is also a type of Christ		

45

The Name

Both the Hebrew and Greek titles of the book reveal its importance to the Israelites. The Hebrew title, *Haddebharim*, means "the words," picking up on the opening phrase of 1:1, "These are the words which Moses spoke to all Israel."[1] Deuteronomy is a series of farewell sermons from Moses to the Israelites, in which he urged the people to love God, obey His laws, and follow the leadership of Joshua.

The Greek title, *To Deuteronomion Touto*, from which we get the English *Deuteronomy*, means "This Second Law."[2] The book, however, isn't a second Law; it is a restatement and expansion of the Law originally given at Sinai and recorded in Exodus and Leviticus. Deuteronomy "fills in missing elements and gives the spiritual significance of the history found in the other books of Moses."[3] During this time of transition, Moses urged a new generation of Israelites to obey God's Law in a new land that had no regard for it.

> "What great nation is there that has statutes and judgments as righteous as this whole law which I am setting before you today?" (Deut. 4:8)

The Setting

Knowing *where* the Jews received these words is crucial to understanding the significance of *what* was said. Moses gave his sermons in the land of Moab (1:5), just across the border from Canaan. Forty years earlier the Hebrews had walked out of Egypt. They received God's laws, even heard His voice. They stood on the brink of Canaan at Kadesh-barnea—then tragically chose not to trust their God who had brought them out of slavery. Now, this next generation stands at the gates of the land promised to Abraham hundreds of years earlier. And they, too, are urged to keep the covenant with God.

This represented a new era in the life of Israel. A new land. A new leader, Joshua. A new way of living—settled instead of nomadic. But the God who brought them here remained unchanged. He was still holy, still faithful, still jealous for the devotion of His

1. Bruce Wilkinson and Kenneth Boa, *Talk Thru the Old Testament*, vol. 1 of *Talk Through the Bible*, (Nashville, Tenn: Thomas Nelson Publishers, 1983), p. 37.

2. Wilkinson and Boa, *Talk Thru the Old Testament*, p. 37.

3. Wilkinson and Boa, *Talk Thru the Old Testament*, p. 39.

people. Now more than ever, on the border of this land whose inhabitants preferred their own gods, the Israelites needed to hear from the one true God.

The Duration of Instruction

Were Moses' messages just a few, quick pep talks? Or were they given over a prolonged period of time? Well, let's do some math. Moses began his first address on "the first day of the eleventh month" (1:3). The Israelites crossed the Jordan on "the tenth of the first month" (Josh. 4:19). Using thirty-day months, that's seventy days. But we need to subtract the thirty days the Israelites mourned for Moses after his death (Deut. 34:8). Moses, then, addressed the Israelites over a period of about forty days, assuming he died shortly after he delivered his last sermon, which is reasonable from the flow of the narrative in Deuteronomy 34.

Forty days to reflect on the past. The miraculous deliverance from Egypt and rescue from Pharaoh's army. God's provision of manna and water in the desert. The bodies of disobedient parents and grandparents who lay buried under desert sand.

Forty days to hear afresh God's own laws for His own people. The Ten Commandments. The holy statutes. The compassionate decrees. The distinctive codes of behavior that would make Israel shine like a city set on a hill.

Forty days for the Israelites to anticipate the realization of God's promises. A land of their own. God's law to guide them . . . and His strength to sustain them.

The Theme

In addressing his fellow Israelites, Moses obviously hoped to stir up their love for God and prolong His influence into future generations.

> "Hear, O Israel! The Lord is our God, the Lord is one! And you shall love the Lord your God with all your heart and with all your soul and with all your might. And these words, which I am commanding you today, shall be on your heart; and you shall teach them diligently to your sons and shall talk of them when you sit in your house and when you walk by the way and when you lie down and when you rise up." (Deut. 6:4–7)

In other words, "Godliness starts here —with this generation.

Love God. Live God. Let every pore of life fill to the brim with His reality. And you will be blessed in the land."

These verses confirm that godliness was never intended to be an add-on activity for the people of God. Rather, godliness is a deep well that waters all of life.

What Moses Wanted Them—and Us—to Remember

Deuteronomy exhorts us to remember at least three essential characteristics about God: His faithfulness, His holiness, and His promises.

Remember God's Faithfulness: Chapters 1–4

"Hindsight is twenty-twenty." Ever use that phrase? It means that we learn a lot by looking behind us. The memory of an event often provides a better perspective than we had when we actually went through it. That's especially true in the spiritual life. When we stop to reflect on the ground we've covered, we see that it's God who got us this far. We remember His faithfulness when we doubted, His strength when we faltered, His grace when we disobeyed.

That's why Moses recounts the journey of the Israelites as they stand on the border of the Promised Land. In this new territory full of idols and detestable practices, forgetting God's faithfulness would be spiritual suicide. Now more than ever, they need to know God is with them. So Moses reminds them:

> "The Lord your God has blessed you in all that you have done; He has known your wanderings through this great wilderness. These forty years the Lord your God has been with you; you have not lacked a thing." (2:7)

When was the last time you stopped to reflect on God's faithfulness throughout your spiritual journey? You might be surprised at how a few moments of reflection can refuel you for the journey ahead.

Remember God's Holiness: Chapters 5–26

Beginning in chapter five, Moses restates God's Law and exhorts his flock to holy living. And for good reason. A whole generation has passed since the original giving of the Law. Of all those who came out of Egypt, everyone over twenty years of age, except for

Moses, Joshua, and Caleb, died in the wilderness. Many in this new generation were small children when the Law was first read; others were not yet born at that time. Though the Law certainly would have been read during the wilderness wanderings, this transitional time called for a renewed commitment by the Israelites to live by God's Law and model His holiness.

Old Testament lecturer Mary Evans helps us appreciate God's Law.

> The requirements of the Law involved every part of life. The regulations cover anything from dealing with serious criminal offenses like murder or rape, to apparently trivial points like allowing a passing walker to eat grapes from a vineyard but not to take any away. There are rules about relations between [masters and servants], the correct way to worship, money management, and the right kind of diet. These rules involve both individuals and the nation as a whole. There is no distinction between religious and secular regulations. If his people were to represent God and show the world what he was like, they had to do so all the time in every area.[4]

Three key lessons stand out from this section. First, *blessings accompany obedience*. God longed to see His loved and chosen people thrive and prosper.

> "Oh, that their hearts would be inclined to fear me and keep all my commands always, so that it might go well with them and their children forever!" (5:29 NIV; see also 6:17–19; 7:12–16; 11:13–15)

God had promised to give the land to the Israelites. So in one sense, their possession of it was unconditional. But their enjoyment of it, their prospering in it, and the constancy of God's blessings were all conditional upon their obedience to His law.

Conversely, a second lesson teaches us that *consequences follow disobedience*.

> "Beware, lest your hearts be deceived and you turn away and serve other gods and worship them. Or

4. Mary J. Evans, "The Message of Deuteronomy," in *The Bible for Everyday Life* (Grand Rapids, Mich.: William B. Eerdmans Publishing Co., 1996), p. 58.

the anger of the Lord will be kindled against you, and He will shut up the heavens so that there will be no rain and the ground will not yield its fruit; and you will perish quickly from the good land which the Lord is giving you." (11:16–17)

Obeying God isn't always easy, is it? The world's table is spread before us, replete with tantalizing dishes like fortune, fame, power, and pleasure. They look and smell so good. But their satisfaction is only temporary. Eventually, if not immediately, the consequences of indulging in them will come. Obeying God is always the best choice. And with His Spirit living in us and His Word to guide us, He has given us everything we need in order to obey.

One final lesson emerges from this section: *Compromise weakens distinctives.* God called Israel to be a distinctive nation among other nations. They were to be holy, light among the darkness, reflecting the very character of God.

> For you are a people holy to the Lord your God. The Lord your God has chosen you out of all the peoples on the face of the earth to be his people, his treasured possession. (7:6 NIV; see also 4:5–8)

The more they became like other nations, though, the less they would resemble God . . . and the dimmer their beacon of hope would shine among the pagan peoples (see 7:1–5).

Remember the Blessings and Warnings of God: Chapters 27–34

The book comes to a close with God's promise to be with the Israelites in the new land and either bless them (28:1–14) or curse them (vv. 15–68)—depending on how well they obey His commandments. He pointedly reminds them:

> "Take to heart all the words I have solemnly declared to you this day, so that you may command your children to obey carefully all the words of this law. They are not just idle words for you—*they are your life.*" (32:46–47 NIV, emphasis added)

The last four chapters mark the end of Moses' ministry among the Israelites. In a final, soul-stirring address to his flock, the man of God bursts into praise to God and blesses the people he has led for forty years.

Moses' ministry ends as it began, with God and him conversing on a mountain. As leadership transitions to Joshua, Moses takes in a breathtaking view of the Promised Land. Though spectacular, it is a mere shadow of where he is going—to heaven, the ultimate Promised Land. And there he will be met, not by a burning bush, but by the great "I Am" in all His blazing splendor. Home . . . at last.

<hr />

This day I call heaven and earth as witnesses against you that I have set before you life and death, blessings and curses. Now choose life, so that you and your children may live and that you may love the Lord your God, listen to his voice, and hold fast to him. For the Lord is your life. (30:19–20a NIV)

 ## Living Insights

And so ends the Pentateuch, the five books of Moses. As you reflect on your study so far, which characteristics of God have stood out most vividly? His sovereignty? His grace? His mercy, perhaps? How about His holiness? Or His faithfulness?

_____

_____

_____

Have these first five books of the Bible taught you anything about God that you didn't know before? Have they emphasized one or more of His attributes in a way that has drawn you closer to Him? How so?

_____

_____

_____

What have you learned about yourself? Your level of trust in God, for example? How well you handle transition? How about your understanding of or your appreciation for Christ's work on the cross?

Take some time to record your thoughts as they come to mind.

_____

_____

_____

Finally, what are you doing to keep track of God's faithfulness in your life? You might want to try keeping a journal. Then, in the days ahead, you'll be able to say with the psalmist,

> Bless the Lord, O my soul;
> And all that is within me, bless His holy name.
> Bless the Lord, O my soul,
> *And forget none of His benefits;*
> Who pardons all your iniquities;
> Who heals all your diseases;
> Who redeems your life from the pit;
> Who crowns you with lovingkindness and
>   compassion;
> Who satisfies your years with good things,
> So that your youth is renewed like the eagle.
> (Ps. 103:1–5, emphasis added)

Chapter 7

JOSHUA: TRIUMPH AFTER TRAGEDY

A Survey of Joshua

His mentor, Moses, was dead.

And now Joshua, by God's grace and power, would lead the new generation of Israelites across the Jordan into the land God had promised to Abraham and his descendants seven centuries earlier. No more wandering. It was time for the Israelites to take what was rightfully theirs by God's decree.

But that meant war. It meant conquest. It meant, as always, that they must trust in God's strength instead of their own. And the most powerful weapon against the pagan nations entrenched in Canaan would not be swords or spears or even numbers. But faith. Faith in the King who "reigns over the nations" (Ps. 47:8).

Introductory Matters

Before following the Israelites across the Jordan River, let's pause to take in some background information.

Title of the Book

The book of Joshua is named after its central figure, Joshua son of Nun. Moses' servant from the time of the Exodus (see Exod. 17; Num. 11:28), he was originally named Hoshea, meaning "salvation," but was rechristened by Moses as Joshua, meaning "the Lord is salvation" (see Num. 13:16). Bruce Wilkinson and Kenneth Boa highlight the significance of this meaning:

> His name is symbolic of the fact that although he is the leader of the Israelite nation during the conquest, the Lord is the Conqueror.[1]

Interestingly, the shortened form of his name in Hebrew has as

---

1. Bruce Wilkinson and Kenneth Boa, *Talk Thru the Old Testament*, vol. 1 of *Talk Thru the Bible* (Nashville, Tenn.: Thomas Nelson Publishers, 1983), p. 52.

JOSHUA

Commissioning the Leader Preparing the People	Conquering the Enemy	Dividing the Spoil			Warning the Victors
Invasion of Land	Subjection of Land	Distribution of Land			The Conclusion
	CENTRAL CAMPAIGN	PHASE ONE	PHASE TWO	PHASE THREE	
The commission (1) The spying (2) The Jordan (3) The memorials (4) The consecration (5)	Jericho (6) Defeat at Ai (7) Victory at Ai (8) Gibeonites (9)	Reuben, Gad, ½ Manasseh (13) Caleb's auto- biography (14) Judah (15) Ephraim (16) ½ Manasseh (17)	Benjamin (18) Simeon, Zebulun, Issachar, Asher, Naphtali, Dan, Joshua (19)	Cities of refuge (20) Levites — 48 towns (21)	Separation (23) Service (24)
	Southern campaign (10) Northern campaign and survey (11) Summary by kings (12)			Civil war threat (22)	
CHAPTERS 1–5	CHAPTERS 6–9 / CHAPTERS 10–12	CHAPTERS 13–17	CHAPTERS 18–19	CHAPTERS 20–21 / CHAPTER 22	CHAPTERS 23–24

Main Theme	Obedient faith brings abundant blessing
Key Verses	1:8; 24:14–15
Christ in Joshua	Typified by Joshua, a victorious leader whose name means "Yahweh is salvation"; pictured in Rahab's scarlet cord, which symbolizes safety through Christ's blood

54

its Greek equivalent *Iesous*—Jesus. Commentator C. J. Goslinga picks up on this.

> Joshua's work and name pointed beyond himself to one greater than he. Joshua was merely a shadow of Him who was to come. But even as a shadow he was permitted to bear the image of the perfect Joshua, our Lord Jesus Christ, who as the "author of their salvation" (Heb. 2:10) triumphed over all the enemies of His people so that He might lead them into the land of eternal rest, the heavenly Canaan.[2]

Date and Authorship

Working ahead from the date of the Exodus, we can determine with reasonable accuracy that the book of Joshua was completed around 1400 B.C. There's no reason to argue against Joshua's authorship. As Goslinga writes, "Joshua's close involvement in nearly everything recounted is a strong reason for ascribing its factual content largely to his own verbal or written reports."[3] Some of the events, however, such as Joshua's death (24:29–33), would have been recorded by someone else, possibly a personal scribe.

Key Words and Ideas

The word *possession* in various forms appears a dozen times in the book. Joshua represents the end of the wilderness wanderings and the beginning of life in Canaan. The Israelites move from promise to possession, from anticipation to occupation, from vagrancy to victory.

However, as Arthur Lewis writes in his introduction to the book of Joshua:

> Joshua is not an epic account of Israel's heroic generation or the story of Israel's conquest of Canaan with the aid of her national deity. It is rather the story of how God, to whom the whole world belongs, at one stage in the history of redemption reconquered a portion of the earth from the powers of this

---

2. C. J. Goslinga, *Joshua, Judges, Ruth*, trans. Ray Togtman, Bible Student's Commentary series (Grand Rapids, Mich.: Zondervan Publishing House, Regency Reference Library, 1986), p. 10.

3. Goslinga, *Joshua, Judges, Ruth*, p. 11.

world that had claimed it for themselves, defending their claims by force of arms and reliance on their false gods. It tells how God commissioned his people, under his servant Joshua, to take Canaan in his name out of the hands of the idolatrous and dissolute Canaanites (whose measure of sin was now full; see Ge 15:16). . . .

The battles for Canaan were therefore the Lord's holy war, undertaken at a particular time in the program of redemption. . . . The conquered land itself would not become Israel's national possession by right of conquest, but it belonged to the Lord.[4]

Prominent themes, then, are (1) faith in God, not man, which is shown in the many miraculous solutions only God could bring about; (2) obedience to God, underscored especially in Achan's story (chap. 7); and (3) the faithfulness of God—He keeps His promises, judges His enemies, and preserves His people with absolute perfection.

Explanatory Survey

Victory comes in stages. Similarly, the book of Joshua unfolds in gradual degrees of conquest and settlement. Basically, the book divides into two main sections. The first half (1:1–13:7) describes the seven-year conquest of the land. The second half (13:8–24:33) gives the details of the division and settlement of the land. From here we can further divide the book into four stages: invasion (chaps. 1–5), subjection (chaps. 6:1–13:7), distribution (chaps. 13:8–22:34), conclusion (chaps. 23–24).

Invasion of the Land: Chapters 1–5

God doesn't do anything haphazardly, including conquering nations. So before the Israelites could enter Canaan, God had to prepare them. He started with their leader, Joshua.

Commissioning the leader (chap. 1). Imagine that you're Joshua. Moses is gone. Before you crossed into Canaan, what would you be thinking? Would you be frightened? Unsure of your leadership

---

4. Arthur Lewis, in *The NIV Study Bible*, ed. Kenneth Barker and others (Grand Rapids, Mich.: Zondervan Bible Publishers, 1985), p. 290.

abilities? Would you be worried that the people would blow it again and wander *another* forty years in the wilderness? Whatever your worries, insecurities, and inhibitions, you would need to hear most of all that God was with you. What an encouragement, then, it must have been for Joshua to hear these words from God:

> "Moses My servant is dead; now therefore arise, cross this Jordan, you and all this people, to the land which I am giving to them, to the sons of Israel. Every place on which the sole of your foot treads, I have given it to you, just as I spoke to Moses. . . . No man will be able to stand before you all the days of your life. Just as I have been with Moses, I will be with you; I will not fail you or forsake you." (Josh. 1:2–3, 5)

Three times in the following verses God urged Joshua to "be strong and courageous" (vv. 6, 7, 9). Courage, though, is always to be guided by obedience, as God made clear to His new general:

> "Be careful to do according to all the law which Moses My servant commanded you; do not turn from it to the right or to the left, so that you may have success wherever you go. This book of the law shall not depart from your mouth, but you shall meditate on it day and night, so that you may be careful to do according to all that is written in it; for then you will make your way prosperous, and then you will have success." (vv. 7b–8)

Once commissioned and committed to following the Lord, Joshua began to prepare the people to enter Canaan. He organized them, reminded them of God's faithfulness, and called them to obedience (vv. 10–15). The people responded by pledging themselves to Joshua's leadership (vv. 16–18).

Preparing the people (chaps. 2–5). In preparing to enter the land, Joshua needed to know what resistance to expect from the Canaanites. So he dispatched spies to scope out the Promised Land, "especially Jericho" (2:1), since it lay directly in their path and was strategic for gaining access to all of Canaan.[5]

5. Notice that he sent them "secretly" (v. 1), perhaps to avoid another incident of national grumbling as occurred at Kadesh-Barnea (see Num. 13).

The spies found refuge with Rahab, a prostitute whose home was on the city wall. Because she had protected them out of respect for the Lord, they promised to spare her and her family during the invasion. (Remember Rahab, for you'll see her again when we get to Matthew—she's one of Jesus' ancestors!)

After the spies returned, Joshua had the people consecrate themselves, because they were about to see God act in a mighty way on their behalf. As He had at the Red Sea, God now parted the Jordan River and led the people across on dry land. This time the Israelites weren't fleeing the Egyptians; they were marching into the Promised Land.

Once they were on the other side and had commemorated their crossing, God commanded Joshua to "circumcise again the sons of Israel the second time" (5:2). By applying this sign to those who didn't yet have it, and by doing it on the threshold of the Promised Land, God was reaffirming His covenant with the descendants of Abraham and expressing His faithfulness to keep His promises. Their celebration of Passover with Canaan in sight would also have impressed upon their hearts God's faithfulness, protection, and deliverance (vv. 10–11).

Subjection of the Land: Chapters 6:1–13:7

This next section highlights both God's power in battle and the necessity to trust Him for true victory. The most stunningly glorious episode is the battle of Jericho, where God toppled the city walls with only the shouts and trumpet blasts of His obedient people (chap. 6).

The most staggeringly tragic incident occurred when the Israelites presumed their next victory, not seeking the Lord first (chap. 7). If they had, they would have learned that Achan had disobeyed God's command to dedicate Jericho's plunder to God alone and instead had taken some for himself. Disobedience and victory do not go hand in hand. When sin is taken care of, though, God's people can accomplish God's plans with His blessings.

Chapters 8–11 record Israel's other key victories, including the day the sun stood still (chap. 10); and chapter 12 catalogues the defeated kings and conquered territories of Canaan. But the victory was not complete. Many Canaanites remained alive and would pose a threat to the Israelites, both spiritually and militarily, in the future (13:1–7).

Distribution of the Land: Chapters 13:8–22:34

Joshua, by now "old and advanced in years" (13:1), set out to divvy up the land according to the tribes' inheritance, with the help of Eleazar the priest and the heads of the tribes (14:1). Author Karen Lee-Thorp describes this section of Joshua:

> Caleb's family requested its portion and set off enthusiastically to wrest it from the enemy. The rest of Judah showed up for its allotment, but those clans were much less successful in taking their property because they trusted Yahweh less, so they decided to cut their losses and settle down among the Canaanites. . . . The tribes of Joseph took the same attitude and even grumbled about the measly portion they were getting. . . . Finally, Joshua practically had to drag the other tribes to allot and move into their lands. Conquest was just too much work, or too scary, and it was easier to tolerate Canaanite neighbors. . . .
>
> This is just what Yahweh had warned against. Living as neighbors would lead soon enough to intermarriage, then intermingling of religions, and eventually to a debasing of Israel's morals.[6]

Conclusion: Chapters 23–24

Conquest, but not complete. Victory, but not total. Joshua knew the risk Israel faced, and in his parting words to his people (possibly the most familiar words in all the book), he did his best to keep them on track.

> "Now, therefore, fear the Lord and serve Him in sincerity and truth; and put away the gods which your fathers served beyond the River and in Egypt, and serve the Lord. And if it is disagreeable in your sight to serve the Lord, choose for yourselves today whom you will serve: whether the gods which your fathers served which were beyond the River, or the gods of the Amorites in whose land you are living; but as for me and my house, we will serve the Lord." (24:14–15)

6. Karen Lee-Thorp, *The Story of Stories*, rev. ed. (Colorado Springs, Colo.: NavPress, 1995), pp. 85–86.

With heartfelt enthusiasm, the people vowed they would always serve the Lord, eagerly submitting to the covenant Joshua made with them that day in Shechem (vv. 16–26). Soon after, Joshua died at the age of 110; then Eleazar the priest, Aaron's son, died also (vv. 29, 33).

Would Israel remain true to her covenant? The disappointing answer is found in the Bible's next book, Judges.

 Living Insights

Do you ever feel as though you're outside the scope of God's love and grace? Ever wonder if He might disown you when you sin? If so, you need to meet Rahab of Jericho.

Not only was Rahab a Canaanite, part of an immoral culture that God wanted to expunge from the Promised Land, she was a prostitute. Yet the Bible tells us that God smiled on her and brought her into His family. By hiding the Israelite spies, Rahab demonstrated her fear of God (Josh. 2:11) and her faith in Him (Heb. 11:31). More astounding than this, she's part of the messianic line, listed in the genealogy of Jesus Christ (Matt. 1:5)!

Her story is a testimony to God's grace, and it is rich with the imagery of Christ Himself. The scarlet cord, for example, that Rahab hung outside her window (Josh. 2:18–21) symbolizes the protection we have from God's judgment under the blood of Christ. In her case, since her house was built into the city wall, her window would have been visible by the Israelite army as they circled Jericho before the walls fell. Through the scarlet cord, Rahab was marked by God not only to be spared from death but to be brought into His covenant family.

So the next time you wonder if God still cares about you, remember Rahab. And remember that God chose us to be His own, that He has saved us from His judgment, and that we are eternally part of His family.

Chapter 8

JUDGES:
RECYCLED MISERY
A *Survey of Judges*

W ith the triumphal strains of Joshua slowly fading in the night, we enter the dark, discordant refrain of Judges . . . definitely a movement in a minor key.

Joshua's final passage sounded this melody: "And Israel served the Lord all the days of Joshua and all the days of the elders who survived Joshua, and had known all the deeds of the Lord which He had done for Israel" (24:31). Judges, however, begins with this disheartening prelude:

> And all that generation also were gathered to their fathers; and there arose another generation after them who did not know the Lord, nor yet the work which He had done for Israel.
> Then the sons of Israel did evil in the sight of the Lord, and served the Baals, and they forsook the Lord. (Judg. 2:10–12a)

What happened? What brought about such a drastic shift?

It seems that even God's own nation wasn't immune to a sequence of destruction that has proved common to many of the world's great civilizations:

From bondage to spiritual faith,
From spiritual faith to great courage,
From great courage to liberty,
From liberty to abundance,
From abundance to leisure,
From leisure to selfishness,
From selfishness to complacency,
From complacency to apathy,
From apathy to dependency,
From dependency to weakness,
From weakness back to bondage.

JUDGES

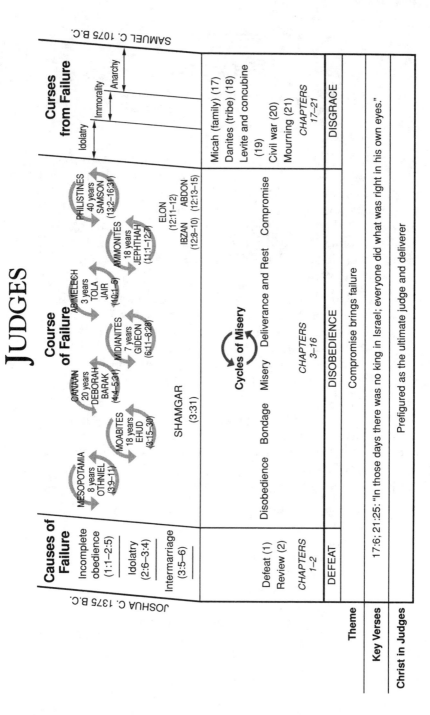

	Causes of Failure	Course of Failure	Curses from Failure
	JOSHUA C. 1375 B.C.		SAMUEL C. 1075 B.C.
	Incomplete obedience (1:1–2:5) Idolatry (2:6–3:4) Intermarriage (3:5–6)	MESOPOTAMIA 8 years OTHNIEL (3:9–11) MOABITES 18 years EHUD (3:15–30) CANAAN 20 years DEBORAH BARAK (4:4–5:31) MIDIANITES 7 years GIDEON (6:11–8:28) ABIMELECH 3 years TOLA JAIR (10:1–5) AMMONITES 18 years JEPHTHAH (11:1–12:7) ELON (12:11–12) IBZAN ABDON (12:8–10) (12:13–15) PHILISTINES 40 years SAMSON (13:2–16:31) SHAMGAR (3:31) **Cycles of Misery** Disobedience Bondage Misery Deliverance and Rest Compromise	Idolatry — Immorality — Anarchy Micah (family) (17) Danites (tribe) (18) Levite and concubine (19) Civil war (20) Mourning (21)
	Defeat (1) Review (2) *CHAPTERS 1–2*	*CHAPTERS 3–16*	*CHAPTERS 17–21*
	DEFEAT	DISOBEDIENCE	DISGRACE
Theme	Compromise brings failure		
Key Verses	17:6; 21:25: "In those days there was no king in Israel; everyone did what was right in his own eyes."		
Christ in Judges	Prefigured as the ultimate judge and deliverer		

62

Dark as this time in Israel's history was, God has chosen to preserve it for a reason. So let's open this book—and our hearts—to receive the lessons recorded there.

Introductory Facts

The name "Judges" refers to the strong leaders God raised up to deliver His people from oppression and lead them in justice.[1] Their stories form the central core of this book, detailing the rescue and rest they brought to Israel for more than three hundred years. The period of history recorded in Judges ranges from about 1380 or 1375 B.C. to between 1075 and 1045 B.C. It probably wasn't written, however, until sometime between the start of Saul's reign and David's capture of Jerusalem (2 Sam. 5:6–10).[2] Though we don't know for certain who the author is, many commentators believe Samuel or one of his contemporaries had a hand in compiling and writing the book.

Judges presents a striking contrast with the book of Joshua. The following chart sketches out some of the major differences between these eras.

Joshua	*Judges*
Joy and achievement	Sorrow and failure
Strength	Weakness
Victory	Defeat
Unity and order	Disunity and anarchy
Freedom	Bondage
Obedience	Disobedience
Conquering	Maintaining
Zeal	Indifference
Consecration	Degradation

One of the major themes emerging from Judges is *failure through compromise.* From passively tolerating the Canaanites' presence in

1. The Hebrew title is *Shophetim,* meaning "judges, rulers, deliverers, or saviors." Bruce Wilkinson and Kenneth Boa, *Talk Thru the Old Testament,* vol. 1 of *Talk Thru the Bible* (Nashville, Tenn.: Thomas Nelson Publishers, 1983), p. 59.

2. Wilkinson and Boa, *Talk Thru the Old Testament,* p. 59.

their Promised Land to actively participating in pagan idolatry and immorality, the tribes of Israel spiraled further and further downward because they wouldn't hold fast to God's Word.

All was not without hope, however. For through all of His people's faithlessness, God still remained faithful. And it was through these people—forgetful, stubborn, disobedient—that the perfectly obedient Messiah would eventually come.

Structural Overview

The book of Judges can be divided into three sections: the prologue (1:1–3:6), the main body (3:7–16:31), and the epilogue (chaps. 17–21). The middle section, and bulk of the book, illustrates Israel's cycles of disobedience and deliverance and also introduces God's chosen judges. The prologue and epilogue act like bookends of misery, emphasizing the melancholy motif of Israel's desertion of God and ultimate degradation. Simply put, Judges opens with disobedience and ends with disgrace.

Let's take a closer look at these sections to understand the book's flow and the author's purpose.

Prologue (1:1–3:6)

The first half of the prologue, chapter 1, details Israel's incomplete conquest of the Promised Land. From verse 19 on through verse 36, we find the tribes of Judah, Benjamin, Ephraim, Manasseh, Zebulun, Asher, Naphtali, and Dan failing to drive out the people occupying the land of their inheritance—as the Lord had commanded.

In chapter 2, the angel of the Lord pronounces judgment on the people for failing to keep their end of the covenant with God (vv. 1–5). Then, from verses 2:6–3:6, we have in a concise summary the cycles of misery and mercy and misery again that we will encounter throughout the rest of the book.

The Main Body (3:7–16:31)

"The sons of Israel did what was evil in the sight of the Lord. . . . Then the anger of the Lord was kindled against Israel, so that He sold them into the hands of . . . When the sons of Israel cried to the Lord, the Lord raised up a deliverer. . . . Then the land had rest" (3:7–11). Seven times in this main section we find this basic pattern.

No region of Israel was exempt from these cycles. Rebellion is first recorded in the south, then travels through the north, the central regions, the east, back to the north, and finally to the west. As Bruce Wilkinson and Kenneth Boa point out,

> Judges gives a geographical survey of apostasy to illustrate its spread and a chronological survey to illustrate its growing intensity.[3]

The chronology of Judges is traced through the deliverers God raised up to help His people. Let's take a moment to get to know them a little. (The major judges are in boldface.)[4]

- **Othniel** (3:7–11): Caleb's nephew and Israel's first judge, Othniel saved his people after eight years of oppression under the king of Aram. During his rule, the land had peace for forty years.

- **Ehud** (3:12–30): Ehud, a left-handed man, delivered Israel from eighteen years of servitude to Eglon, the king of Moab (a story definitely worth reading!). Ehud's legacy was eighty years of peace for his people.

- Shamgar (3:31): Possibly serving during Othniel's or Ehud's time, Shamgar is noted for killing six hundred Philistines single-handedly, his only weapon an oxgoad.

- **Deborah** (chaps. 4–5): The only woman judge, Deborah went into battle with Barak, a warrior who would only go into combat if Deborah would fight with him. She delivered her people from twenty years of Canaanite oppression. Her triumph, and that of Jael, the woman who killed the enemy commander, is commemorated in song in chapter 5. Deborah provided peace for forty years.

- **Gideon** (chaps. 6–8): Gideon is probably best remembered for his testing of the Lord with the sign of the fleece—he first requested that it be wet and the ground dry, then that the fleece would be dry but the ground wet. The Lord graciously obliged him and used Gideon's three hundred-man army to route the Midianites, who had oppressed Israel for seven years. Wanting

---

3. Wilkinson and Boa, *Talk Thru the Old Testament*, p. 60.

4. Some people include Barak as a judge, serving in conjunction with Deborah, as well as Abimelech, Gideon's son, who appointed himself king over Shechem.

to make him their king, the people heard this much-needed response from Gideon: "I will not rule over you, nor shall my son rule over you; the Lord shall rule over you" (8:23). Through him God gave the land forty years of peace.

- Tola (10:1–2): Following Abimelech's reign of terror (he was Gideon's son, and he obviously didn't heed his father's words), Tola saved Israel and judged his people for twenty-three years.

- Jair (10:3–5): Jair was noted for having "thirty sons who rode on thirty donkeys," probably a sign of wealth. He judged Israel twenty-two years.

- **Jephthah** (10:6–12:7): An illegitimate son cast out of his father's family, Jephthah was called back by his townspeople to rescue them from the Philistines and Ammonites—who had oppressed God's people for eighteen long years. A foolish vow on his part cost him his only child, his daughter; and foolish pride on the part of the Ephraimites cost them 42,000 men at Jephthah's army's hands. He judged Israel only six years.

- Ibzan (12:8–10): A judge of Israel for seven years, he is primarily remembered for having thirty sons and thirty daughters.

- Elon (12:11–12): Elon, from the tribe of Zebulun, judged Israel for ten years.

- Abdon (12:13–15): Abdon, another wealthy man, judged Israel eight years and had "forty sons and thirty grandsons who rode on seventy donkeys" (v. 14).

- **Samson** (chaps. 13–16): The last judge chronicled in the book of Judges, Samson is probably the best known. Unfortunately, he is often remembered more for his lust than for delivering his people from the Philistines, the oppressors of Israel for forty years. He judged Israel twenty years, though he killed more of his people's enemies at his death than he did in his life.

The conclusion of Samson's story also concludes the main body of Judges. From here we enter the disturbing epilogue, which provides examples of the nation's immorality that still shock after all these hundreds of years.

The Epilogue (Chapters 17–21)

Chapters 17–18 record the thievery and idolatry of Micah, as well as the corruption of a Levite priest who sells his services to the highest bidder. Chapter 18 ends with the slaughter of a peaceful town, Laish. Chapters 19–21 tell of the appalling gang rape and murder of a Levite's concubine, the subsequent civil war against the tribe of Benjamin for not dealing with the men who committed the heinous crime, the slaughter of the people of Jabesh-gilead, and the kidnapping of four hundred virgins from that city.

Most commentators believe that these events took place much earlier in the chronology of Judges but were placed at the end to emphasize the nation's fall from God's glorious promise. The last verse is the key verse of this book:

> In those days there was no king in Israel; every-
> one did what was right in his own eyes. (21:25)[5]

Theme Explored

Such bright promise and possibility was theirs through God's blessings; yet instead of choosing life, the Israelites chose death and reaped the whirlwind of God's curses (see Deut. 28:15–68). Why did they do this? How did it all come about? If we go back to the beginning of the book, we'll be able to trace the reasons.

Reasons for Failure

First of all, as we saw in the prologue, *their obedience was incomplete*. They did not drive out the pagan inhabitants of the land as God had told them to (Judg. 1:19–36). And slowly but surely, they began to take on the ways of the peoples around them; *they accommodated idolatry* (2:10–13, 17–19). Once they were assimilated into the pagan culture, they took the next step down and *they intermarried with pagans* (3:5–6). How hard it is to love God when your heart belongs to someone who doesn't value Him.

God had left the Canaanites in the land to teach the Israelites how to fight (3:1–2); but He also left them there to test His people and see if their hearts were truly His (2:21–23). They clearly failed that most important test.

Cycles of Misery

The key that unlocks this book comes in 2:11–19, where the five-step cycle of misery is first presented. Here we find

5. This theme surfaces three other times in chapters 17–21: in 17:6; 18:1; and 19:1.

(1) disobedience (vv. 11–13), (2) bondage (v. 14), (3) misery (v. 15), (4) deliverance and rest (vv. 16, 18), and last (5) compromise (vv. 17, 19).

Disgrace in Society

Returning to the epilogue, we see God's people turn away from Him and reach out instead to idols—both shrines and money. Doing what was right in their own eyes, rather than God's, they swiftly turned to the worst forms of immorality. With their immoral, self-seeking selves as their standard, they knew no unity, only anarchy.

Concluding Warnings

Judges may be ancient history, but human nature is still the same. Three timeless lessons emerge from the darkness of this account.

First, *depravity results in permissiveness when righteousness is ignored.* The daily newspapers testify to this. If we ignore righteousness long enough, depravity will breed permissiveness—which allows us to feel right about doing something wrong.

Second, *permissiveness leads to rationalization when holiness is ignored.* When holiness is no longer the standard, sin gets redefined rather than honestly dealt with.

Third, *rationalization encourages rebellion when repentance is ignored.* Personal responsibility vanishes when wrong gets massaged into right.

Though Judges ends on a bleak note, all was not lost. In the Bible's next book, Ruth, we find a story of loyalty, love, and honor that took place during the era of the judges. Here is a picture of God at work behind the scenes, even playing matchmaker for a couple who will become part of the Messiah's line.

 Living Insights

How relevant a book is Judges! It shows both the absolutely unchangeable standards God wants us to live by as well as His mercy to repentant hearts.

In your family, are you teaching God's standards and His mercy to your children? Do they appreciate the beauty and blessing of holy living? Or when they cheat on a test, act mean to the dog, tell "a little white lie," or sleep with their boyfriend or girlfriend, is that rationalized away, shrugged off with a "God understands we're only human" mentality?

The generation entering the Promised Land with Joshua was told by Moses to "teach [God's commandments] diligently to your sons" (Deut. 6:7). But if you'll look at Judges 2:10, you'll find that somehow the godly generation of Joshua's time didn't seem to teach the next generation about God: "There arose another generation after them who did not know the Lord, nor yet the work which He had done for Israel."

Parents, grandparents, aunts, uncles, cousins—teach the children in your family who God is and how wonderful His ways are. Teach by word and deed, from Scripture and from your own life. Teach the principles behind the rules. Yes, there will come a time when they will make their own choices. But at the very least, with your input they will be more inclined to choose the ways of life over the ways of death (Deut. 30:15–20).

Chapter 9

RUTH: INTERLUDE OF LOVE

A Survey of Ruth

The period of the judges—with all its apostasy, bloodshed, divine discipline, and miraculous deliverance—is the last place one would expect to find a love story. But if you listen carefully, somewhere behind the cacophony of Judges you can hear the love ballad of Ruth softly playing.

It's a human love story, to be sure. But it's much more than that. It's a story of God's unfailing love for His covenant people and how He brought a foreigner into that covenant—a Moabite woman named Ruth. God not only honored and blessed her but also included her as an integral link in redemption history.

If we'll endeavor to understand the book of Ruth, we'll appreciate more deeply the love, care, and sovereignty of God. And we'll be encouraged that we can walk with God and experience His blessings, even when everything around us tempts us to walk another way.

Introduction

Ruth's story takes place during the time of the judges (1:1). Remember the very last verse of the book of Judges? It summarizes the spiritual climate of that era:

> In those days there was no king in Israel; everyone did what was right in his own eyes. (Judg. 21:25)

God repeatedly rescued His people from destruction through such leaders as Ehud, Deborah, and Gideon. But the Israelites still followed their own passions and preferences, ignoring the Law of God. They simply had not learned that true blessing comes by following the Lord.

Conversely, the lives of Ruth, Naomi, and Boaz shine through the dismal period of the judges like a shaft of sunlight through a steel-gray sky. Through their story, God shows once again that He will always maintain a remnant of His righteousness in the world,

RUTH

	Ruth's Choice	Ruth's Service	Ruth's Claim	Ruth's Marriage
	NAOMI AND RUTH (Mutual grief)	RUTH AND NAOMI AND BOAZ (Mutual pursuit)		BOAZ AND RUTH (Mutual love)
	"May the Lord grant that you may find rest." (v. 9)	"Naomi had a kinsman . . . whose name was Boaz." (v. 1)	"Wait . . . until you know how the matter turns out.'" (v. 18)	"Boaz took Ruth, and she became his wife." (v.13)
	CHAPTER 1	CHAPTER 2	CHAPTER 3	CHAPTER 4
Setting	"Now it came about in the days when the judges governed that there was a famine in the land."			
Circumstance	Loss—deeper commitment		Gain—deeper love	
Emotion	Grief	Loneliness	Companionship	Rejoicing
Main Theme	Redemption: God provides for those who trust Him in hard times			
Key Verses	1:16; 3:11–12			
Christ in Ruth	Prefigured in the kinsman-redeemer			

no matter how evil that world becomes. His kingdom, as Martin Luther wrote, is forever.

Ruth: A Life of Faith

Ruth's response to life's difficulties is a model of faith and trust in God. This is an amazing fact, considering that she was a non-Jew, a woman no one would have expected to trust so completely in the God of Israel.

Chapter 1: Ruth's Choice

The story begins with hunger: there's a famine in Israel. The Promised Land has become parched and empty. How can this be? Did not God Himself describe Canaan as "a land flowing with milk and honey" (Exod. 3:8)? Indeed He did. But He also warned Israel that their agricultural and societal abundance depended on their spiritual obedience (see Deut. 28). Since they had ignored God's law and degenerated into spiritual famine, a physical famine followed—just as God had predicted.

Bethlehem, which means "house of bread," was now a house without bread. So four of its inhabitants—a hard-working Israelite, his wife, and two sons—left in search of food. They traveled to Moab, thirty-five miles southeast of Bethlehem, on the other side of the Dead Sea.

Elimelech, the father, died in the new land, leaving Naomi a widow. But the dream of coaxing crops from foreign soil stayed alive in her two sons. They married Moabite women, Orpah and Ruth, and remained in Moab for ten more years.

Then tragedy struck again. Naomi's two sons, Mahlon and Chilion, died. She was left with her two daughters-in-law . . . and no one to work the soil and provide for the family. Now Naomi's soul was as empty as her stomach had been when her family first arrived in Moab. Had this all been for nothing? she must have wondered. Would she have been better off to have stayed in Bethlehem and taken her chances?

When she heard that the famine had finally subsided, Naomi set off for Bethlehem. She urged Orpah and Ruth to return to their Moabite families, where they would be provided for and might even remarry. Orpah did return, but Ruth clung to her mother-in-law. She only knew two things, but they were enough. She knew she loved Naomi, and she knew there was a God in Israel. So faithful

72

Ruth and empty Naomi returned to Bethlehem.

What a scene! Who would have blamed Ruth if she had gone back to her family? Certainly not Naomi. Yet Ruth had committed herself to this family. And she would rather go to a strange land with Naomi than stay in Moab without her. That's commitment. That's trusting God in the midst of pain. Ruth made the hard choice . . . but the right choice.

At the end of chapter 1, the writer gives us a hint that God will honor Ruth's choice:

> And they came to Bethlehem at the beginning of barley harvest. (1:22b)

Chapter 2: Ruth's Service

Though grieving, Naomi and Ruth knew life had to go on. So Ruth went to work in the fields, picking up scraps left behind by the harvesters ("gleaning"). In her years of living in a Hebrew family, Ruth had apparently learned of God's mercy on the poor and destitute. Perhaps she had even read the law itself, which prescribed:

> "When you reap your harvest in your field and have forgotten a sheaf in the field, you shall not go back to get it; it shall be for the alien, for the orphan, and for the widow, in order that the Lord your God may bless you in all the work of your hands." (Deut. 24:19; see also Lev. 19:9–10; 23:22)

By "chance," the field in which she gleaned belonged to Boaz, a relative of Elimelech's. Kind and hospitable, Boaz invited her to stay and work in his field until the end of the harvest. He even invited her to sit and eat with him—and he instructed his reapers to deliberately leave behind some grain for Ruth to collect (Ruth 2:16).

When Ruth took the day's grain home to Naomi and told her where she had gleaned, Naomi recognized Boaz's name. "That man is our close relative," she said, probably unable to contain her joy. "He is one of our kinsman-redeemers" (2:20 NIV).

What is a kinsman-redeemer, and why would Naomi be so excited that Ruth had met him? The kinsman-redeemer

> was responsible for protecting the interests of needy members of the extended family—e.g., to provide

an heir for a brother who had died (Dt 25:5–10), to redeem land that a poor relative had sold outside the family (Lev 25:25–28), to redeem a relative who had been sold into slavery (Lev 25:47–49) and to avenge the killing of a relative (Nu 35:19–21).[1]

No wonder Naomi was overjoyed. Once empty and without hope, she was beginning to see how God might fill her again. Through Boaz, Naomi and Ruth could be provided for, their land could be kept in the family, and their lineage could continue.

Chapter 3: Ruth's Claim

Having seen God's hand in Boaz's involvement, Naomi took the next step. She advised Ruth to approach Boaz and appeal to his position as kinsman-redeemer (3:3–4). His positive response would mean not only a husband for Ruth but the possibility to honor the memory of her husband and sons.

So, after putting on her best clothing and perfume, Ruth went to the threshing floor where Boaz was winnowing the grain and celebrating the harvest.[2] While he slept, she "uncovered his feet and lay down" (3:7). That is, she took the part of his blanket that covered his feet and draped it over herself. This gesture, as C. J. Goslinga explains,

> had a symbolic meaning. By sharing the same blanket with Boaz, Ruth made known that she was claiming the place of his wife; but her position at his feet signified that she did not yet have that status. Before that could happen, Boaz himself had to acknowledge her right. Naomi probably also told Ruth what to say, but the most important thing was that she listen to Boaz's advice. As an upright Israelite with a sincere

1. Marvin R. Wilson, John H. Stek, "Ruth," in *The NIV Study Bible*, ed. Kenneth Barker and others (Grand Rapids, Mich.: Zondervan Bible Publishers, 1985), p. 367.

2. Grain was winnowed after it was threshed. After it had been beaten from the stalks and lay mixed with the chaff on the threshing floor, the two were thrown upward with the winnow; and the chaff was blown away by the evening wind, leaving only the grain behind. This work seems to have been done by the landowner himself, who then would sleep the night on the threshing floor (a large, open area where the ground had been stamped hard) to guard his harvest. C. J. Goslinga, *Joshua, Judges, Ruth*, trans. Ray Togtman, Bible Student's Commentary series (Grand Rapids, Mich.: Zondervan Publishing House, Regency Reference Library, 1986), p. 536.

respect for justice and law, he certainly would know the right thing to do.[3]

A single woman approaching a sleeping man in the dark. Does this seem a little forward? A bit indiscreet? Some scholars have tried to make a case for immorality in this passage, but nothing in the text suggests this. Commentator John W. Reed says:

> [Ruth's] mother-in-law had complete confidence in the integrity of the kinsman-redeemer. Boaz could be trusted to act responsibly. And Ruth was recognized by everyone as "a woman of noble character" (v. 11). The uncovering of the feet was a ceremonial act that was completely proper. Probably the scene took place in the dark so that Boaz had the opportunity to reject the proposal without the whole town knowing about it.[4]

Ruth had a legitimate desire for a husband. And she had a right under Jewish law, as a relative of Elimelech's, to approach a kinsman-redeemer. So she showed no impropriety. She followed Naomi's instructions, acted according to the law, and won the respect and admiration of Boaz. She was available . . . but careful. Responsive . . . but pure.

Boaz responded with joy to Ruth's plea. But one more hurdle remained. There was another relative closer to Naomi than Boaz. The law required that he be given first choice as redeemer. This was the perfect opportunity for Ruth and Boaz to let their feelings determine their action. "Forget the law!" they could have said. "I love you; I don't want to take my chances on anyone else." But they realized that gaining a blessing by ungodly means was no blessing at all. Though interested in one another, they were patient. They trusted God.

Chapter 4: Ruth's Marriage

Boaz and Ruth, rather than rushing into marriage, waited for God to confirm that their desires matched His will. So Boaz

3. Goslinga, *Joshua, Judges, Ruth*, p. 537.

4. John W. Reed, "Ruth," in *The Bible Knowledge Commentary*, Old Testament edition, ed. John F. Walvoord and Roy B. Zuck (Wheaton, Ill.: Scripture Press Publications, Victor Books, 1985), pp. 424–25.

presented Naomi's other relative with the opportunity to buy Elimelech's property and bring Naomi and Ruth into his household.

The other kinsman-redeemer, however, declined. Apparently, he was willing to purchase the land. But the fact that Elimelech had no offspring meant that this nearer relative must count Ruth's first son as an heir of Elimelech's.

> When [the nearer redeemer] learned from Boaz that Ruth owned the property along with Naomi (v. 5), he knew that if Ruth bore him a son, that son would eventually inherit not only the redeemed property but probably part of his own estate too. In that sense the nearer redeemer would "endanger" his estate. However, if only Naomi were the widow (not Naomi *and* Ruth), then no son from the levirate marriage would inherit part of the redeemer's estate because Naomi was past childbearing.[5]

Upon the other relative's refusal, Boaz chose to redeem the land and Ruth. He had trusted God all along and didn't have the same reservations about endangering his estate that the nearer relative had.

Boaz and Ruth approached marriage with complete trust in God. They followed His law, they maintained purity, and they moved ahead with confidence as God opened doors. They glorified Him in their romantic desires. And the result? God not only blessed them, but blessed Naomi . . . and us.

A Feast for Naomi

Remember Naomi? God did. Once empty, she was now full. Life, once bitter, tasted sweet again. Bethlehem, the "house of bread," had indeed become a place of satisfaction and nourishment for her soul. God had provided her with a kinsman-redeemer, a loving daughter-in-law, and the joy of a grandson. A grandson whose line would produce the ultimate Kinsman-Redeemer. For Obed, the child, was the grandfather of King David. And from David's line came the Messiah, Jesus Christ Himself—the Bread of Life who fills our famished souls.

5. Reed, "Ruth," pp. 426–27.

Living Insights

One of the most profound lessons in Ruth's story just might be the grace of God. Because we're all Ruths and Naomis, really. At least we were before we met Jesus. Like Ruth, we were foreigners. We didn't know God. In fact, we were His enemies. And like Naomi, we were empty spiritually. But the Great Kinsman-Redeemer purchased us from sin's hold and brought us into His family. The Babe from Bethlehem, the "house of bread," has filled us with the Bread of Life and satisfied our souls.

What qualities of God do you see in the book of Ruth that encourage you in your personal walk with Him?

_____

_____

_____

What doubts, anxieties, or feelings of hopelessness do you experience that the book of Ruth speaks to?

_____

_____

_____

In what ways has God "filled" you?

_____

_____

_____

What areas do you need to trust Him to fill?

_____

_____

_____

Chapter 10

1 SAMUEL: NATION IN TRANSITION

A Survey of 1 Samuel

Author Karen Lee-Thorp, in her book *The Story of Stories*, transitions from Ruth to 1 Samuel this way:

> About the time Ruth and Boaz were happily raising Obed, another wife was suffering the curse of barrenness less than thirty miles north. Her husband's other wife teased her to the point that Hannah was praying desperately for a baby. When Yahweh finally gave her a son, she was so grateful that she dedicated him to serve at the tabernacle as soon as he was about three years old. She gave him into the care of Eli, the priest in charge.[1]

And so began the life of Samuel. As both prophet and judge, Samuel occupied a unique place in Israel's history. As Israel's last judge, he is a key transition figure. Samuel shepherded the nation from a theocracy to a monarchy and installed her first king, Saul. As prophet, he annointed and counseled kings, and spoke God's word to a nation bent on going its own way.

First Samuel, the first of two books that bear Samuel's name, chronicles his rise to prominence, Saul's forty-year rule, and David's time as king-in-waiting. Through the lives of these three men, 1 Samuel teaches us about trust, obedience, and the necessity of taking God seriously.

Background on 1 Samuel

Before starting our journey through 1 Samuel, let's see how this book fits into Scripture's overall story.

Place in Biblical History

The two books of Samuel existed originally as a single literary

---

1. Karen Lee-Thorp, *The Story of Stories*, rev. ed. (Colorado Springs, Colo.: NavPress, 1995), p. 92.

1 SAMUEL

	Samuel The Last Judge				Saul The First King		Beginning Samuel's godliness National hope Motivation Purity	ENDING Saul's apostasy Depression Personal despair Suicide
	BIRTH	GROWTH AND CALL	MINISTRY	CHANGE	REJECTION BY GOD Impatient Rash Disobedient "Insane" Jealous Murderous	REBELLION AGAINST GOD DAVID chosen, trained, tested, protected . . .		
	CHAPTER 1	CHAPTERS 2–3	CHAPTERS 4–7	CHAPTERS 8–12	CHAPTERS 13–16	CHAPTERS 17–31		
Attitude of the People	Public trust				Public disillusionment			
Main Theme	Though leaders and nations change, God's purposes always move forward							
Key Verses	8:6–9; 13:14							
Christ in 1 Samuel	Typified in Samuel, who was a prophet, priest, and judge; also portrayed in the life of David . . . shepherd, king, and born in Bethlehem							

79

work, as did 1 and 2 Kings and 1 and 2 Chronicles. These were all subsequently divided into paired books by the translators of the Septuagint (the Greek version of the Hebrew Bible).

First Samuel spans the time from Samuel's birth to the end of Saul's reign, a period of about ninety-four years (c. 1105–1011 B.C.).[2] Second Samuel covers the reign of David, which lasts about forty years. First and 2 Kings recount Solomon's reign and Israel's split into two nations, tracing the rule of the kings of Israel and Judah (almost four hundred years). The Chronicles virtually ignore the northern kingdom of Israel, focusing instead on Judah and the messianic dynasty of David.

Author

The book of 1 Samuel does not reveal its author, but as Bruce Wilkinson and Kenneth Boa state,

> Jewish talmudic tradition says that it was written by Samuel. Samuel may have written the first portion of the book, but his death recorded in First Samuel 25:1 makes it clear that he did not write all of First and Second Samuel. Samuel did write a book (10:25), and written records were available. As the head of a company of prophets (see 10:5; 19:20), Samuel would be a logical candidate for biblical authorship.[3]

Summary of 1 Samuel

Because this book recounts Israel's transition from judgeship to kingship, we can easily divide the book by the nation's last judge, Samuel, and her first king, Saul.

Chapters 1–12 spotlight Samuel—his birth (chap. 1), his call and service under Eli (chaps. 2–3), his leadership over Israel (chaps. 4–7), and his supervision of the transition to the monarchy (chaps. 8–12).

Samuel's speech in chapter 12 is the bridge that carries us into the reign of Saul. The rest of the book, chapters 13–31, traces the triumph and tragedy of Israel's first king. Saul is appointed by God, then rejected by Him for his disobedience (chaps. 13–16). The final section chronicles Saul's continued rebellion against God, his

2. Bruce Wilkinson and Kenneth Boa, *Talk Thru the Old Testament,* vol. 1 of *Talk Thru the Bible* (Nashville, Tenn.: Thomas Nelson Publishers, 1983), p. 71.

3. Wilkinson and Boa, *Talk Thru the Old Testament,* p. 71.

jealous pursuit of David, and, finally, his death by his own hand (chaps. 17–31).

Though David figures prominently in chapters 16–30, his story is told within the framework of Saul's rise and fall. David's reign is the focus of 2 Samuel.

To get a firmer grasp of what 1 Samuel is all about, let's delve deeper into the lives of the book's two major characters.

Samuel: Israel's Last Judge

Appropriately, 1 Samuel begins with the story of Samuel's entrance into the world.

Samuel's Birth (Chap. 1)

We have already met Samuel's mother, Hannah, and seen God's mercy in response to her anguished prayers. When her baby was born, she named him Samuel, which means "heard by God." When he was weaned, about age three for Hebrew children, mother and son made the fifteen-mile trek to Shiloh.

Hannah brought two sacrifices to the tabernacle that day—a bull for slaughter and a son for service. She offered both with joy, for God had turned her barrenness into blessing. Now Samuel would be a blessing to others by serving in the tabernacle and speaking on behalf of the Lord.

Samuel's Faithful Service and Special Call (Chaps. 2–3)

The tabernacle at that time desperately needed some godly representation. Eli the priest had two sons, also priests, who were "worthless men; they did not know the Lord" (2:12). Instead of offering the sacrificial meat to the Lord, they gorged themselves on the choicest portions. They also defiled the tabernacle by having sex with the women who served there. Eli, though disapproving of his sons' activities, did little to stop them. His passivity resulted in God's judgment on his family.

In the midst of all this carnality, Samuel grew in spirit and stature, serving faithfully in the Lord's house. While God marked Eli's family for judgment, He blessed Samuel's. Hannah had five more children. And at the appointed time, God spoke to young Samuel, publicly confirming him as His prophet (see 3:19–21).

Samuel's Leadership of Israel (Chaps. 4–7)

Though Samuel faithfully spoke God's words, Israel didn't always listen. As in the days of Joshua and the judges, the people wavered in their commitment to the Lord. Such disobedience gave Israel's enemies the upper hand in battle.

After losing four thousand men to the idolatrous, warlike Philistines, Israel next lost the sacred ark of the covenant to them. For the next seven months, however, the ark caused nothing but trouble for Israel's enemies. So, reeling from the heavy hand of God's judgment—which showed itself in the destruction of their god and in an affliction of painful tumors—the Philistines sent the ark back to Israel.

But the Israelites' defeat of the Philistines would not happen simply because the ark was returned. *Israel* had to return to the Lord. And Samuel showed them the way.

> Then Samuel spoke to all the house of Israel, saying, "If you return to the Lord with all your heart, remove the foreign gods and the Ashtaroth from among you and direct your hearts to the Lord and serve Him alone; and He will deliver you from the hand of the Philistines." (7:3)

The Israelites repented and called on the Lord. And they struck down the Philistines, who would not bother Israel again "all the days of Samuel" (vv. 11–13).

Transition to Monarchy (Chaps. 8–12)

As Samuel grew older, the time came for him to pass the mantle of leadership to another. He hoped it would be to his sons, whom he had already appointed as judges. But his sons were taking bribes—unraveling justice instead of upholding it. What should be done?

The answer, surprisingly, came from the people.

> "Now appoint a king for us to judge us like all the nations." (8:5b)

Even though they were having trouble following their heavenly King, the Israelites wanted an earthly monarch. Perhaps they thought the glint of a golden crown or flowing robes would intimidate the enemy in battle. So God told Samuel, in effect, "They shall have their king. And when they see how poorly he reigns, they'll wish they had stuck with Me."

God then led a Benjamite named Saul to Samuel. He was striking in appearance and towered above his countrymen. Following God's instruction, Samuel anointed him king and presented him to the people, whose hearts he won when he defeated the Ammonites.

The stage was now set for Samuel's farewell, but before leaving, he called both king and subjects to follow their heavenly King . . . or suffer His judgment. With this final warning, Samuel stepped out of the lead and into a supporting role.

Saul: Israel's First King

Saul now took center stage in what would become a tragedy for himself and many who lived under his rule.

God's Rejection of Saul (Chaps. 13–16)

Early in his reign, Saul proved God right. He demonstrated that favorable appearance alone does not make a king. By habitually doing things his way instead of God's, Saul tarnished the crown of Israel—a reminder that the only untarnished crown rests on the head of the King of heaven.

Immediately after offering a prebattle sacrifice at Gilgal—a duty reserved solely for Samuel—Saul was told by the old priest,

> "You have acted foolishly; you have not kept the commandment of the Lord your God, which He commanded you, for now the Lord would have established your kingdom over Israel forever. But now your kingdom shall not endure. The Lord has sought out for Himself a man after His own heart, and the Lord has appointed him as ruler over His people, because you have not kept what the Lord commanded you." (13:13–14)

Saul's impulsiveness and disregard for God's commands continued throughout his reign. A rash vow he made would have taken his son Jonathan's life had not the Israelite army intervened. And he not only disobeyed God's orders to wipe out the Amalekites, he tried to veil his disobedience as a righteous act. God saw through it, however, and Samuel again told Saul,

> "The Lord has torn the kingdom of Israel from you today, and has given it to your neighbor who is better than you." (15:28)

That "neighbor" was David, the shepherd boy from Bethlehem. Though perhaps not as physically impressive as Saul, David had a heart fit for the kingship. God, therefore, sent Samuel to anoint the boy. But it would be some time before he would take the throne. For the time being, David tended sheep and, ironically enough, tended Saul. Whenever the king was troubled in his soul, he would send for the young psalmist to play the harp. Saul would unwittingly serve as the agent who nudged David into Israel's limelight.

Saul's Rebellion against God (Chaps. 17–31)

Chapter 17, like chapter 12, is a pivotal chapter in the book. Here David, on a mission to bring food to his warrior brothers, heard the blasphemous taunts of the Philistine Goliath. Armed with a sling, five smooth stones, and the strength of the Lord, David felled the giant. With the Philistine champion now dead, the Israelites routed their enemies. And the ruddy shepherd boy from Bethlehem was hailed as a hero.

Saul appointed David as his chief warrior and sent him out against Israel's enemies. But when the people praised David over Saul because of his victories—"Saul has slain his thousands, And David his ten thousands" (18:7)—Saul seethed with jealousy. "Now what more can he have but the kingdom?" he fumed (v. 8). And from that day on, "Saul looked at David with suspicion" (v. 9), even trying to run his loyal servant through with a spear while in a demon-induced rage.

The rest of the book narrates Saul's obsession with destroying David and describes David's life on the run from Saul's murderous fury.

> Driven to the wilderness area of Judah, the logical place because of his familiarity with it from childhood, David lived out a "Robin Hood" existence for nearly 10 years. . . . But God was teaching David many things in those days, lessons David still shares with all who read his psalms which find their setting in this turbulent period of his life (see, e.g., Pss. 18; 34; 52; 54; 56–57). All these things were surely working together to prepare David to be the kind of leader who would glorify God and inspire His people.[4]

4. Eugene H. Merrill, "1 Samuel," in *The Bible Knowledge Commentary*, Old Testament edition, ed. John F. Walvoord and Roy B. Zuck (Wheaton, Ill.: Scripture Press Publications, Victor Books, 1985), p. 450.

David moved from city to city to escape Saul's wrath, and Saul followed in bloody pursuit. Yet, although David had two opportunities to kill Saul, he refused to raise his hand against "the Lord's anointed." One man's irrationality only served to highlight the other's integrity.

The book began with the birth of a prophet. It ends with the death of a king. In a battle with the Philistines, a wounded Saul took his own life; and his son Jonathan, David's dear friend, died in the skirmish as well.

> Thus Saul died with his three sons, his armor bearer,
> and all his men on that day together. (31:6)

The King Who Will Not Fail

Saul's story is a tragic one, and it leaves us longing for a better king, one with a heart for God. And that's what we'll find in David's story in 2 Samuel.

But even David only serves to point us toward a king whose crown will never tarnish—Jesus Christ Himself. His reign is incorruptible, His faithfulness unwavering, and His character pure. Earthly kings, presidents, and dictators will come and go. But none can ever replace the righteous rule of our heavenly King.

> O come, let us sing for joy to the Lord;
> Let us shout joyfully to the rock of our salvation.
> Let us come before His presence with
>   thanksgiving;
> Let us shout joyfully to Him with psalms.
> For the Lord is a great God,
> And a great King above all gods,
> In whose hand are the depths of the earth;
> The peaks of the mountains are His also.
> The sea is His, for it was He who made it;
> And His hands formed the dry land. (Ps. 95:1–5)

 Living Insights

Suppose tall, handsome Saul were standing before you and next to him stood little David, the youngest of Jesse's sons. Which one would you want as your king? Whom would you hire to work for

85

your company, lead your church, or promote your ideas? With which one would you rather have your picture taken or be seen in public? In other words, what influences you more: inner character or outward appearance?

Let's admit it. We often put too much stock in how people look. But God sees what really matters. He sees "not as man sees, for man looks at the outward appearance, but the Lord looks at the heart" (1 Sam. 16:7b).

Consider the men and women God has used in building His kingdom. Most weren't that impressive physically. Moses, who had a speech problem, delivered God's ultimatum to Pharaoh. Paul's critics said his "personal presence is unimpressive, and his speech contemptible" (2 Cor. 10:10), yet he penned thirteen books of the New Testament. Leah, one of Jacob's wives, wasn't beautiful like her younger sister, Rachel (Jacob's other wife). Her eyes "were weak," and Jacob despised her and adored Rachel (Gen. 29:17). But God loved Leah and opened her womb. She bore Judah, through whom the Messiah would come (Matt. 1:2).

We wouldn't even have considered Jesus to be one of the "beautiful people," not outwardly anyway.

> He has no stately form or majesty
> That we should look upon Him,
> Nor appearance that we should be attracted to Him.
> (Isa. 53:2)

God seems to delight in using the very people we would pass by. In doing so, He emphasizes that the power to change the world resides in Him, not in human strength.

So keep working on the inner life. Progress of the soul may not be immediately evident to human onlookers. But the soul is where the gaze of God is most tightly focused.

Chapter 11

2 SAMUEL: ECSTASY AND AGONY OF A KING

A Survey of 2 Samuel

Saul was dead by his own sword, an eerily appropriate end for the king whose worst enemy in life was himself.

Now David was free from Saul's maniacal pursuit. Yet upon hearing the news of his king's death, David responded—not with relief or ambition or righteous indignation—but with poetic grief.

> "Your beauty, O Israel, is slain on your high
>   places!
> How have the mighty fallen! . . .
> Saul and Jonathan, beloved and pleasant in their
>   life,
> And in their death they were not parted;
> They were swifter than eagles,
> They were stronger than lions.
> O daughters of Israel, weep over Saul,
> Who clothed you luxuriously in scarlet,
> Who put ornaments of gold on your apparel.
> How have the mighty fallen in the midst of the
>   battle!
> Jonathan is slain on your high places. . . .
> How have the mighty fallen,
> And the weapons of war perished!"
> (2 Sam. 1:19, 23–25, 27)

What a humble, tender, gracious heart David's words reveal. Though thoroughly human and tragically fallible, as we shall see, it is because of his core character that David will always be remembered as "a man after God's own heart" (1 Sam. 13:14; Acts 13:22). He was the standard against whom all the subsequent kings of Judah and Israel were measured. His life not only pictures what true faith—and faltering faith—can be, it reveals a God whose grace and mercy sustains us all.

2 SAMUEL

David's Triumphs			David's Troubles			Appendix
Reigning in Hebron	Reigning in Jerusalem		With	With His	With His	Miscellaneous
Over Judah	Over All Israel		Himself	Family	Nation	Narratives
	A new capital (5)			Amnon's immorality (13)		A famine (21)
	A new worship center (6)			Absalom's crime and flight (14)		A song (22)
	A new dynasty (7)			Absalom's revolt (15)	David's return (19)	A prophecy (23)
David's lament (1)	A new boundary (8)		David's sin (11)	Absalom's counselors (16–17)	Sheba's revolt (20)	A failure (24)
David's crowning (2)	A new son (9)		Nathan's denunciation (12)	Absalom's death (18)		
David's increase (3–4)	Another new boundary (10)					
CHAPTERS 1–4	*CHAPTERS 5–10*		*CHAPTERS 11–12*	*CHAPTERS 13–18*	*CHAPTERS 19–20*	*CHAPTERS 21–24*

Christ in 2 Samuel	Foreshadowed in David's reign, which, though imperfect, is characterized by justice, wisdom, and integrity; the Messiah, the Son of David, is promised as an offspring of the Davidic line and One who will sit upon David's throne forever

Relationship between 1 and 2 Samuel

First and 2 Samuel, remember, were originally one book. It's very likely that part of 1 Samuel was written by Samuel. Some believe the prophets Nathan and Gad might also have had a hand in completing that book and writing 2 Samuel (see 1 Chron. 29:29). Authors Bruce Wilkinson and Kenneth Boa describe the relationship between 1 and 2 Samuel this way:

> First Samuel reveals how the kingdom was established and Second Samuel shows how it was consolidated. This book tells us how the nation was unified, how it obtained Jerusalem as its royal capital, how it subdued its enemies and extended its boundaries, and how it achieved economic prosperity. It records the beginning of an endless dynasty and the life of a man about whom more is known than any other individual in the Old Testament.[1]

Survey of 2 Samuel

With the tragic end of Saul's reign, David's reign began. Their contrasts are striking. Where Saul rejected God, David revered Him. Where Saul sought his own way, David sought the Lord's. And where Saul desperately tried to take what wasn't his, David graciously accepted from the Lord that which had already been promised to him.

But not even David's life was without trouble. He committed adultery and murder. His family, and eventually his kingdom, fell into turmoil.

The major divisions of the book represent the success and moral failure of David. Chapters 1–10 highlight his triumphs; chapters 11–20, his troubles. Chapters 21–24 record some of the king's final words and deeds. David's reign rises to a pinnacle in chapter 10, then slopes down for the rest of the book.

Second Samuel, however, isn't just about one man's life. It demonstrates how the spiritual condition of one person can affect all who follow him.

---

1. Bruce Wilkinson and Kenneth Boa, *Talk Thru the Old Testament*, vol. 1 of *Talk Thru the Bible* (Nashville, Tenn.: Thomas Nelson Publishers, 1983), pp. 79–80.

David's Triumphs (Chaps. 1–10)

Reigning in Hebron (Chaps. 1–4). The book begins by showing David's respect for God's sovereignty. Rather than rejoicing at the news of Saul's demise, David slew the Amalekite who brazenly claimed to have killed the king. Wicked as Saul was, he had been God's anointed ruler; because of that, David refused to assume the monarchy by human means but waited instead on God's perfect timing.

After grieving over Saul and Jonathan, David asked the Lord where he should go. "To Hebron," the Lord replied (2:1). So David, his wives, and the six hundred men and their families who had rallied around him during Saul's persecution traveled twenty miles northeast to Hebron. There the tribe of Judah anointed him king over their territory.

Those loyal to Saul, however, wanted to keep the crown in Saul's family. Abner, commander of Saul's army, installed Saul's son Ish-bosheth as king over the northern tribes. But after a disagreement with him, Abner sought to unite all the people under David. Abner never saw the unification; unknown to David, he was killed by Joab, the commander of David's army, who was avenging his brother's death. Eventually, Ish-bosheth was killed by his own men, who met the same fate as the Amalekite who killed Saul. Despite the unwanted violence, David's path was now clear.

Reigning in Jerusalem (Chaps. 5–10). With their king now dead, the northern tribes looked toward Hebron. They anointed David king over all Israel, recognizing him as God's chosen ruler (5:1–3). David reigned in Hebron for seven and a half years, then he relocated the royal capital north to Jerusalem. The city was a strategic location for the king's residence, not only because it was central to all the tribal territories, but because it proved to be very well fortified. Once settled in Jerusalem, David's family grew, and the Lord granted him victory against Israel's enemies.

Yet Jerusalem still lacked something—the ark of the covenant. It wasn't enough to have a geographical center to the nation; David knew that God's presence was central to Israel's very life. So David set out to retrieve the ark.

Though the ark came to Jerusalem amid great celebration, David had a nagging feeling that something still wasn't quite right. He saw that he lived in a palace of rich cedar, but the ark of God dwelled "within tent curtains" (7:2). So he wanted to build a house for the Lord.

God declined his offer, though; He wanted David's son Solomon, a man of peace, to fulfill that role. Instead, God promised to build *David* a house—a dynasty of kings that would never end (v. 16). Initially, that dynasty would comprise earthly kings. Ultimately, though, David's line would produce the King of Kings, Jesus Christ, to whose kingdom there is no end.[2]

Humbled and overcome with God's grace, David worshiped the Lord—the king bowing before his King.

David continued to prosper under God's blessing. His army seemed invincible, and his territory greatly expanded. Yet he seemed unspoiled by all the success. He demonstrated a heart of generosity and kindness, especially in his gracious treatment of Jonathan's crippled son, Mephibosheth (chap. 9).

This section closes with the Israelites' defeat of the mercenary Arameans, who swore allegiance to Israel after the battle.

There seemed to be nothing King David couldn't acquire—cities, armies, fame. He went too far, though, when he took another man's wife.

David's Troubles (Chaps. 11–20)

Troubles with Himself (Chaps. 11–12). Spring. It's the time "when kings go out to battle" (11:1), when the winter rains subside and the hard work of the harvest has not yet begun. But David remained in Jerusalem. We're not told why. He would have been better off, though, clashing swords with his enemies. For his most difficult battle, one that would eventually cripple his kingdom, waited for him in the ease and comfort of his own palace.

> Now when evening came David arose from his bed and walked around on the roof of the king's house, and from the roof he saw a woman bathing; and the woman was very beautiful in appearance. So David sent and inquired about the woman. And one said, "Is this not Bathsheba, the daughter of Eliam, the wife of Uriah the Hittite?" And David sent messengers and took her, and when she came to him, he lay with her; and when she had purified herself from her uncleanness,[3] she returned to her house. (11:2–4)

2. Second Samuel 7:8–16 is known as the Davidic Covenant, where David's "throne shall be established forever" through a coming Messiah.

3. David and Bathsheba broke the law that forbids adultery, and any ceremonial observance of the law could not erase that fact.

After discovering that Bathsheba was pregnant, David summoned her husband, Uriah, from the battlefront. He tried to persuade the loyal soldier to sleep with his wife, obviously in hopes of making Uriah appear to have fathered the child. Uriah refused to indulge in pleasure, though, even with his wife, knowing that the other soldiers had to sleep out in the open, near the field of battle.

So David sent Uriah back to the battle and ordered him placed on the front lines. He died in combat. Now David was not only guilty of adultery and deceit, but murder.

God, through the prophet Nathan, confronted David with his sin and announced the consequences.

> "'Now therefore, the sword shall never depart from your house, because you have despised Me and have taken the wife of Uriah the Hittite to be your wife.' Thus says the Lord, 'Behold, I will raise up evil against you from your own household; I will even take your wives before your eyes, and give them to your companion, and he shall lie with your wives in broad daylight.'" (12:10–11; see also v. 14)

Though David repented and experienced God's forgiveness (v. 13), his household and his kingdom would experience turmoil for the rest of his days.

Troubles with His Family (Chaps. 13–18). The royal family began to fall apart. The child conceived by David's illicit union with Bathsheba died soon after he was born. David's son Amnon raped his half sister Tamar. Absalom, Tamar's brother, seethed for two years as David did nothing about this crime. Then Absalom finally killed Amnon himself. Another two years passed before David spoke to Absalom.

In the ultimate rejection of his father's authority, Absalom launched a rebellion against David, forcing the king to flee Jerusalem. Absalom even went up to the palace roof and publicly had sex with ten of David's concubines, fulfilling Nathan's terrible prophecy. When the rebellion was finally crushed, Absalom was dead. And David collapsed in grief.

Troubles with His Nation (Chaps. 19–20). The king returned to Jerusalem only to find more dissension among the members of his kingdom. The tribes of Israel and Judah argued over who was favored more by David. Finally, a "worthless fellow" (20:1) named

Sheba, from Saul's tribe of Benjamin, rallied all the tribes but Judah to follow him in rebelling against David. This rebellion was also crushed. But the troubles weren't over.

Appendix (Chaps. 21–24)

The final four chapters of the book focus on various words and deeds of David, which reflect the king's continued seeking after God as he struggled with his own weaknesses.

"In the days of David" (21:1), a three-year famine ravaged Israel. The Lord revealed to David that the famine was a judgment for Saul's violation of a covenant with the Gibeonites—some of whom he killed. To make amends to the Gibeonites, David gave them seven of Saul's descendants, who were hanged for their ancestor's crime.

The famine ended, but war continued with the Philistines. All of the battles recorded in 21:15–22, oddly enough, include giants. They were all killed, but not by David—a sign of the king's age, but perhaps a sign, too, that his glory days were coming to a close.

Chapter 22 is a song of praise David sang to the Lord when God "delivered him from the hand of all his enemies and from the hand of Saul" (22:1). Following the song, David recalls in a poem God's faithfulness to keep His covenant. The names and deeds of David's "mighty men" follow the poem (chap. 23).

The book closes with David's taking a census of the land. This project was apparently motivated by pride and self-sufficiency, for it brought God's judgment. The Lord inflicted Israel with a pestilence, but withdrew it when David repented and intervened with offerings on behalf of his people (chap. 24).

Lingering Lessons

Forty years of kingship—that's a lot of life to look at. What lessons can we take with us?

First, *prosperity and ease can be perilous times*. Material abundance may indeed be a sign of God's blessing. But we can use His good gifts in ways that dishonor Him. The combination of too much money and too much time can be deadly.

Second, *gross sin is the culmination of a process, not a sudden act*. David had seven wives before he married Bathsheba. A godly view of sex can hardly be expected to thrive in such a harem. David's struggle with lust began long before he spotted Bathsheba from his rooftop.

Third, *confession and repentance help heal wounds, but they don't erase scars.* A pastor may be forgiven for his affair with the secretary, but he may never lead a church again. The homosexual saved by God's grace may still die of the AIDS he contracted as a non-Christian. God's forgiveness is always there for us, but the better choice is to avoid sin. Ask David; he knows.

 Living Insights

Did you catch any glimpses of Christ, the "Son of David," in the story of David's life? Did you see the prefiguring of our perfect King, whose kingdom has no end? The ark's celebrated return to Jerusalem may have reminded you that Jesus, even more than the ark, is God's presence among us. What about David's kindness toward Mephibosheth? Did it show you that we, once spiritual cripples, have been permitted to come and sit at the King's table?

As you read through 2 Samuel, what else from David's life prompts you to reflect on God's goodness and grace through Christ?

_____

_____

_____

_____

_____

_____

Chapter 12

1 KINGS: SOLOMON AND A CIVIL WAR
A Survey of 1 Kings

Old and tired, David spent his days trying to keep warm, huddled under a mound of blankets. While he dreamed of days gone by, his son Adonijah schemed to set himself up as king, just as another son, Absalom, had tried to do. Adonijah's rebellion had both military and spiritual support—Joab, the former commander of David's army, and Abiathar the priest were among those shouting, "Long live King Adonijah!"

But God had already chosen David's successor. And almost as soon as Adonijah's celebration had started, it ended. A new cry pulsed through the streets of Jerusalem: "Long live King Solomon!"

Introduction to 1 Kings

First Kings continues the story of Israel's troubled monarchy, tracing the reign of Solomon, the division of the kingdom, and the lives of prophets and kings of both Israel and Judah. At the heart of the book is God's covenant with His people. The various monarchs are presented in light of how well (or how poorly) they lived by God's covenant standards.

First and 2 Kings, like 1 and 2 Samuel and 1 and 2 Chronicles, were originally one book, called simply "Kings" in Hebrew tradition. The author can't be determined with certainty. Jewish tradition credits Jeremiah, while others have suggested Ezra and Ezekiel. Whoever wrote 1 Kings incorporated outside sources into his work, a common practice among biblical writers.[1]

Solomon's Reign (Chaps. 1–11)

The first half of the book displays Solomon in all his splendor: his fame, his wisdom, his wealth. Under his reign, Israel entered a grand, but ultimately tragic, era.

---

1. A few of these sources are listed for us in Scripture: "the book of the acts of Solomon" (11:41), the "Book of the Chronicles of the Kings of Israel" (14:19), and the "Book of the Chronicles of the Kings of Judah" (14:29).

1 KINGS

	Solomon *"In all his splendor"*	Decline and Demise	Disruption *"A kingdom divided against itself"*
POLITICALLY David succeeded by Solomon	Crowned and inaugurated (1–2)		Internal conflict and hostility (12–14)
NATIONALLY Kingdom united	Married and exalted (3–4)		Civil war and idolatry (15–16)
ECONOMICALLY Solid and secure	Temple erected and dedicated (5–8)		Ahab and Elijah (17–22)
SPIRITUALLY Shaky	Warned and blessed (9–10)		"He served Baal and worshiped him and provoked the Lord God of Israel to anger according to all that his father had done." (22:53)
	CHAPTERS 1–10	*CHAPTER 11*	*CHAPTERS 12–22*

POLITICALLY
King after king

NATIONALLY
Kingdom divided

ECONOMICALLY
Unstable

SPIRITUALLY
Empty

Time	Forty years		Eighty years
Kingdom	United and strong		Divided and weak
People	Solomon		Jeroboam to Ahaziah Rehoboam to Jehoshaphat
Identity	"All Israel . . . sons of Israel"		North: Israel; Samaria; Ephraim South: Judah; Jerusalem
Key Verses	9:3–9; 11:11–13		
Christ in 1 Kings	Solomon's wisdom, which foreshadows Him who "became for us the wisdom of God" (1 Cor. 1:30); the prophetic ministry and miracles of Elijah		

96

Solomon's Rise (Chaps. 1–10)

With Solomon anointed and declared king, Adonijah's false reign immediately dissolved. Well aware of the responsibility and the temptations that lay ahead for his young son, David charged Solomon to walk with God so that the Lord would fulfill His promise to David and his family (1 Kings 2:2–4). Having spoken this solemn warning, the shepherd-king "slept with his fathers and was buried in the city of David" (v. 10). After David's death, Solomon punished or killed those who had rebelled against his father. With justice done and old enemies gone, "the kingdom was established in the hands of Solomon" (v. 46).

Chapter 3 opens with Solomon's marriage to Pharaoh's daughter, a political union creating trade advantages for both Israel and Egypt. More importantly, though, this chapter records a crucial dialogue between God and Solomon.

> In Gibeon the Lord appeared to Solomon in a dream at night; and God said, "Ask what you wish Me to give you." Then Solomon said, ". . . Give Thy servant an understanding heart to judge Thy people to discern between good and evil. For who is able to judge this great people of Thine?"
>
> And it was pleasing in the sight of the Lord that Solomon had asked this thing. And God said to him, ". . . Behold, I have given you a wise and discerning heart, so that there has been no one like you before you, nor shall one like you arise after you. And I have also given you what you have not asked, both riches and honor, so that there will not be any among the kings like you all your days." (3:5–6a, 9–11a, 12–13)

God's promise proved marvelously true. After Solomon brilliantly mediated a dispute between two women over the custody of a child, word of his great wisdom spread throughout the known world (4:29–34). His kingdom expanded, and the people of Israel prospered (vv. 20–28).

He next turned his energies to building the house for God that his father had dreamed of (chaps. 5–6). After seven years of construction, the breathtaking structure was complete. (His own palace took thirteen years to build—its splendor surpassed only by the temple's.)

The ark was placed in its midst, and the glory of the Lord filled the temple. Then Solomon led the people in worship with prayer and sacrifice—a religious event as spectacular as the temple itself (chap. 8).

With these building projects completed, God pulled Solomon aside and breathed this solemn reminder: "Be careful; you're not immune to failure. Walk in My ways, and I'll extend your kingdom forever. Turn away from Me, and this whole nation, including My temple, will come to ruin" (see 9:1–9).

For the time being, Solomon walked with God, and God's blessing was evident to all. Even the Queen of Sheba traveled 1200 miles to see if the reports of Solomon's wealth and wisdom were true (10:1–10). In those days, there was no one more famous or more sought after than Solomon.

> So King Solomon became greater than all the kings of the earth in riches and in wisdom. And all the earth was seeking the presence of Solomon, to hear his wisdom which God had put in his heart. (10:23–24)

Solomon soon demonstrated, however, that those whose hearts wander from God can turn even His blessings into tools of self-destruction.

Solomon's Decline and Demise (Chap. 11)

In chapter 11, the hinge of 1 Kings, Solomon slips from fame to failure, from success to sensuality, from temple-builder to idol-worshiper. His spiritual troubles, as with his father David, started at home. Solomon indulged his desires for foreign women—he had "seven hundred wives, princesses, and three hundred concubines" (v. 3a). And they "turned his heart away" from the Lord to worship their false gods (vv. 3b–8).

Solomon discovered, as did his father, David, that sin has consequences.

> So the Lord said to Solomon, "Because you have done this, and you have not kept My covenant and My statutes, which I have commanded you, I will surely tear the kingdom from you, and will give it to your servant. Nevertheless I will not do it in your days for the sake of your father David, but I will tear it out of the hand of your son." (vv. 11–12)

About that time, God tossed a boulder into the placid waters of Solomon's kingdom, raising up enemies from the surrounding lands of Edom and Aram to harass Solomon. From within the kingdom, He summoned Jeroboam, son of Nebat, to rule over ten tribes of Israel, leaving only Judah and Benjamin for Solomon's heir.

A Kingdom Divided (Chaps. 12–22)

The last half of 1 Kings recounts the division of the kingdom into north (Israel) and south (Judah) and the successes and failures of their kings. The picture is not a pretty one. Immorality and idolatry were rampant, as both nations acquiesced to the lifestyles of the surrounding nations and closed their hearts to the desires of God. Of the thirty-nine monarchs between the two nations, Scripture characterizes only eight of them as godly rulers.

Rehoboam and Jeroboam (Chaps. 12–14)

After Solomon's death, his son Rehoboam took the throne. Determined to oppress the people instead of serve them, he unwittingly split the kingdom. Ten of the tribes followed Jeroboam, who set himself up as king over them. Rehoboam remained in Jerusalem to rule over Judah and Benjamin.

Though Jeroboam's reign had been predestined by God, the king immediately turned away from Him when his throne was established in Shechem. Hoping to keep his followers from returning to Jerusalem to worship in the temple, Jeroboam set up golden calves for them to worship. He also appointed his own false priesthood. Because Jeroboam led Israel astray, God promised to wipe his lineage from Israel.

Judah fared no better. During Rehoboam's reign, Judah sacrificed on "the high places," built idols, and engaged in temple prostitution.

Kings of Judah

After Rehoboam was "buried with his fathers in the city of David" (14:31), his son Abijam (also known as Abijah, see 2 Chron. 13:2) became king. He reigned only three years, and his brief era is summed up in 1 Kings 15:3: "He walked in all the sins of his father."

His son Asa, however, walked in the ways of his great-great-grandfather: "Asa did what was right in the sight of the Lord, like

David" (v. 11). He got rid of the male cult prostitutes and the idols of his father, and he removed the queen mother from her powerful role because of her idolatry. The high places remained, however, but Scripture tells us, "nevertheless the heart of Asa was wholly devoted to the Lord all his days" (v. 14).

In verse 24, we read that Asa's son Jehoshaphat took the throne after the death of his father. But, significantly, the narrative of 1 Kings drops the history of Judah and veers into the degeneration of Israel until chapter 22. There we pick up the thread of Jehoshaphat's story again and find that he was a good king like his father, even though the people "still sacrificed and burnt incense on the high places" (22:43).

Judah's history in 1 Kings ends with Jehoshaphat's son Jehoram ascending the throne.

Kings of Israel

Meanwhile, back in chapter 15, we see the beginning of Israel's long line of wicked kings. Notice that Israel has no dynasty of kings coming from one family, as does Judah. Many of Israel's kings took the throne through murder.

- Nadab, Jeroboam's son who reigned two years and "did evil in the sight of the Lord" (v. 26), was murdered by Baasha.

- Baasha wiped out every descendant of wicked Jeroboam, but he still followed idols and "did evil in the sight of the Lord" throughout his twenty-four-year reign (vv. 33–34).

- Elah, Baasha's wicked son, was next on the throne, ruling for two years. While he was drunk, one of his military commanders killed him (16:8–10).

- Zimri, Elah's assassin, next wiped out all of Baasha's line. His seven-day reign ended when Omri, the commander of Israel's army, besieged the royal city. In cowardice, Zimri set fire to the king's house and burned himself in it (vv. 11–20).

- Tibni tried to take the throne from Omri, who had already been declared king when Zimri usurped the throne (v. 16). Omri prevailed, and Tibni died (vv. 21–22).

- Omri reigned twelve years and earned the distinction of acting "more wickedly than all who were before him" (v. 25). He established Samaria as the capital of Israel and installed an even more wicked king on the throne after him: his son Ahab (vv. 28–30).

Ahab and Elijah (Chaps. 17–22)

When we reach the last six verses of chapter 16, we understand why the previous couple of chapters focused more on Israel than on Judah. Like the crash of cymbals after a swelling crescendo, Ahab is the climax of evil in 1 Kings.

> Ahab did more to provoke the Lord God of Israel
> than all the kings of Israel who were before him.
> (v. 33)

God is not one to leave His people in darkness, however. With the faithlessness of King Ahab came the faithfulness of the prophet Elijah.

In chapter 17, Elijah stood eye-to-eye with Ahab and declared that God would cause a drought and a resulting famine in Israel because of Ahab's wickedness. God then hid His prophet at the brook Cherith, where the ravens miraculously brought him food. When the brook dried up, Elijah headed north to Zarephath to live with an impoverished widow and her son. He was a channel of God's mercy to this woman: like the fishes and the loaves in Jesus' hands, this woman's flour and oil kept multiplying through Elijah's promise. And when her young son died, Elijah prayed to God three times, and He brought the boy back to life.

In chapter 18, Elijah sought out Ahab and challenged the prophets of Baal to a showdown. On Mount Carmel, 450 frenzied Baal worshipers were soundly defeated by the true God of Israel and were slain by Elijah. Afterward, Elijah told Ahab that the drought was over and he'd better run for cover from the coming storm. Jezebel, however, enraged over the defeat of her prophets, threatened Elijah that *he'd* better run for cover because she was going to kill him (19:1–2).

Chapter 19 shows us that even the bravest of prophets weren't immune from fear, as Elijah fled for his life. In the wilderness of Beersheba, God nurtured His despondent servant and showed Him that His presence is not always in a blasting wind, an earthquake, or a fire but is sometimes in "a sound of a gentle blowing" (v. 12). Gently, the Lord reminded Elijah that he wasn't battling Ahab alone, and He even provided him with a companion and protégé, Elisha.

Chapter 20 details a war between Ben-hadad and Ahab, who, like Saul before him, disobeyed God and let the enemy king live. When rebuked by God's prophet, Ahab became "sullen and vexed" (v. 43)—his mood foreshadowing the dark events of chapter 21.

Here he coveted a vineyard belonging to Naboth the Jezreelite. When Naboth wouldn't sell, Ahab pouted and Jezebel plotted. She arranged to have Naboth falsely accused and stoned to death so that her husband could take possession of Naboth's vineyard. Elijah again confronted the wicked king, saying, "Thus says the Lord, 'In the place where the dogs licked up the blood of Naboth the dogs shall lick up your blood, even yours'" (21:19).

In chapter 22, Ahab went to war to reclaim the city of Ramoth-gilead. He talked Jehoshaphat, king of Judah, into fighting with him; but then he disguised himself for battle, leaving Jehoshaphat as the only one to look like a king—and a target. God was not fooled, however. A "certain man drew his bow at random," hit Ahab, and the king bled to death in his chariot. When his servants washed the blood away, the dogs came and licked it up (vv. 34–38), just as Elijah had prophesied.

After Ahab's death, his son Ahaziah took the throne, "and he did evil in the sight of the Lord" (v. 52).

And so ends 1 Kings . . . sorrowfully distant from the glory days of David.

Applicational Highlights

Four lessons for application linger from this book. First, *unchecked sinful bents are passed from parent to child.* Rehoboam learned idolatry from Solomon. Solomon learned about lust from David. What are we teaching our children? Our kids are watching, whether we realize it or not.

Second, *we are most vulnerable to temptation when we least expect it.* Solomon fell at the height of his success. And so can we. Past spiritual and material achievements do not guarantee future faithfulness. We must constantly depend on God's guidance and protection.

Third, *God always has the right person to match the hour.* There will always be Jeroboams and Ahabs. But God always has an Asa or Elijah waiting in the wings. No matter how great the wickedness of this world, God will not allow the light of His righteousness to be snuffed out.

Fourth, *when life seems especially dark, God comes especially close.* God specializes in turning darkness into light, hopelessness into hope, defeat into victory. Need proof? There's an empty tomb in Jerusalem . . . and a full throne in heaven.

 ### *Living Insights*

Kingdoms. Covenants. Nations. Eternity. All of these are under God's control. But make no mistake. His panoramic view of redemptive history doesn't cause Him to miss even the slightest detail of human need.

God removes one kingdom from power and sets up another, yet He never forgets that kingdoms are made of people. People like the widow from Zarephath, broken with grief over her son's death. Through the prophet Elijah, God restored the boy to life, and his mother to joy (1 Kings 17:17–24).

God isn't like so many human fathers who lose touch with the people in their lives because they're preoccupied with work. He doesn't miss a single detail. Jesus put it this way:

> "Look at the birds of the air, that they do not sow, neither do they reap, nor gather into barns, and yet your heavenly Father feeds them. Are you not worth much more than they?" (Matt. 6:26)

Which details of your life do you need to trust Him with today?

_____

_____

_____

_____

_____

_____

_____

_____

_____

Chapter 13

2 KINGS: FROM
COMPROMISE TO CAPTIVITY

A Survey of 2 Kings

God keeps His word.

It seems like a long time since we read the covenant God made with His people in Deuteronomy. Maybe that covenant seemed a long ways off to the Jews in the era of the kings too. But where the passing of time can fade our memories and erode the promises we make, it has no effect on God. And He was about to keep a certain promise He had declared to His people through Moses.

> If you do not obey the Lord your God and do not carefully follow all his commands and decrees I am giving you today, all these curses will come upon you and overtake you . . .
> The Lord will drive you and the king you set over you to a nation unknown to you or your fathers. . . . You will become a thing of horror and an object of scorn and ridicule to all the nations where the Lord will drive you. (Deut. 28:15, 36–37 NIV; see also vv. 49–57, 64–68)

God had set before His people life and death, blessings and curses. As we have seen in 1 Kings, and as we'll see in 2 Kings, both Israel and Judah repeatedly and stubbornly chose the curses. Because of their persistent disobedience, God gave them what they chose: captivity.

"The kingdom divided in First Kings," write Bruce Wilkinson and Kenneth Boa, "becomes the kingdom dissolved in Second Kings. God's patience is long; God's pleading is persistent; but when ignored, God's love can also be severe."[1]

Let's follow the continuing stories of Israel and Judah, taking to heart their hard lessons so we can avoid a similar spiritual catastrophe in our own lives.

---

1. Bruce Wilkinson and Kenneth Boa, *Talk Thru the Old Testament*, vol. 1 of *Talk Thru the Bible* (Nashville, Tenn.: Thomas Nelson Publishers, 1983), p. 91.

2 KINGS

	Northern Kingdom Israel	Both Kingdoms (Alternating)	Southern Kingdom Judah
	CHAPTERS 1–10	CHAPTERS 11–17	CHAPTERS 18–25
Northern Prophets	Elijah Elisha	Jonah Amos Hosea	
Southern Prophets		Obadiah Joel Micah Isaiah	Nahum Zephaniah Jeremiah Habakkuk
Northern Kings	Ahazian to	Hoshea	
Southern Kings		Jehoram to	Zedekiah
Main Theme	God is patient, but He does not allow persistent sin to go unpunished		
Key Chapters	17 and 25		
Christ in 2 Kings	Foreshadowed in the faithfulness of some Judean kings; seen in the healing ministry and compassion of Elisha		

ISRAEL'S FALL TO ASSYRIA 722 B.C.

JUDAH'S FALL TO BABYLON 586 B.C.

Structure of 2 Kings

Second Kings, like 1 Kings and the Chronicles, can be hard to follow. It's chock-full of names and dates, places and events—often given in rapid fire. It's helpful to understand that the author of 2 Kings

> systematically traces the reigning monarchs of Israel and Judah, first by carrying one nation's history forward, then retracing the same period for the other nation.[2]

The first ten chapters give prominence to people and events in Israel, the northern kingdom. Chapters 11–17 alternate between Israel and Judah, until Israel falls to Assyria in chapter 17. The last section, chapters 18–25, follows Judah and her kings until their deportation to Babylon.

Emphasis on the Northern Kingdom (Chaps. 1–10)

Ahab's son Ahaziah inherited not only his father's evil ways but also the prophet who wouldn't let his father off the hook.

Elijah and Ahaziah (Chaps. 1–2)

After an injury that led to a lingering illness, Ahaziah sought supernatural help—but not from the God of Israel. What he got, though, was God's prophet Elijah, a divine rebuke, and death instead of recovery (2 Kings 1). Jehoram (also known as Joram), Ahaziah's younger brother, succeeded Ahaziah as king of Israel.

In chapter 2, another succession took place. In contrast to the Lord's abandonment of Ahaziah, He sent "a chariot of fire and horses" to take Elijah up "by a whirlwind to heaven" (v. 11). Like Enoch before him (see Gen. 5:24), Elijah was one of two people in all history to escape death. The mantle of prophet then passed to Elijah's apprentice, Elisha, whose ministry is highlighted from here through chapter 8.

Elisha (Chaps. 2–13)

God wasted no time in putting Elisha to work. Here are a few highlights from his ministry.

- Through Elisha, God filled with oil the empty jars of a poor

2. Wilkinson and Boa, *Talk Thru the Old Testament*, p. 92.

widow, which she sold to pay her creditors and keep her sons out of slavery (4:1–7).

- He asked God to grant a Shunnamite's desire for a child; and when the boy later died, he raised him from the dead (vv. 8–37).

- He multiplied loaves to feed the people—just as Jesus would do in His own ministry (vv. 42–44; see also Matt. 14:13–21; 15:32–38).

- He healed Naaman, an Aramean captain, of leprosy (2 Kings 5:1–19).

- He secured the merciful treatment of Israel's captured enemies (6:8–23).

True peace, however, never settled in Israel, as chapter 8 shows. Elisha prophesied future conflict between Aram and Israel (v. 12), while Judah struggled with Edom (v. 22).

Judah's evil King Jehoram married Athaliah, Ahab's daughter, and after his death, their son Ahaziah briefly took the throne. Meanwhile, in Israel, Ahab's dynasty was about to be wiped out.

Jehu (Chaps. 9–10)

Chapters 9 and 10 relate the story of Jehu, whom Elisha anointed king over Israel. Jehoram, Ahab's son, however, was still on the throne. But Jehu was God's choice—not only to take the throne but to destroy what remained of Ahab's line, thus fulfilling God's prophecy of that dynasty disappearing (see 1 Kings 21:20–29).

Jehu performed his bloody duty with precision and cunning, assassinating both King Jehoram of Israel and his nephew, King Ahaziah of Judah. By the end of Jehu's killing spree, the household of Ahab, including his evil wife, Jezebel, was all but obliterated. Jezebel's death was even more grisly than her husband's yet just as prophetically accurate (compare 1 Kings 21:23 with 2 Kings 9:30–37). Next, Jehu scraped Israel clean of Baal worship, although he was "not careful to walk in the law of the Lord, the God of Israel, with all his heart" (10:31).

Alternating Accounts of Both Kingdoms (Chaps. 11–17)

Ahab's dynasty was gone in Israel. So, his daughter Athaliah attempted to preserve that dynasty in Judah by seizing the throne for herself and annihilating David's line.

Queen Athaliah of Judah (Chap. 11)

The death of her son Ahaziah cleared the way for Athaliah to declare herself queen and slaughter any rightful heirs to David's throne. Her wrath almost sears the page like flames.

The Lord, however, intervened to preserve the line of Judah: Athaliah's grandson Joash was taken away by his aunt Jehosheba and hidden. Kept safe during Athaliah's six-year reign, Joash was publicly declared king at age seven. The queen was executed (chap. 11).

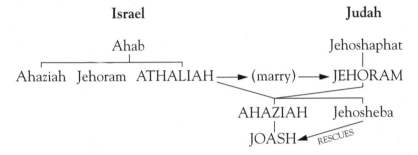

Joash of Judah (Chap. 12)

Overall, in 2 Kings Joash (also called Jehoash) is considered a good king, even though "the high places were not taken away" (12:3). He did repair the temple, though, which had been neglected during Athaliah's, his father's, and his grandfather's reigns. Joash, along with the priest Jehoiada, removed Baal worship from Judah. Thomas L. Constable points out the importance of his reign.

> The beginning of Joash's reign marks the commencement of over 100 years of consecutive rule by four men who were all judged as good kings. None of these four—Joash, Amaziah, Azariah (Uzziah), and Jotham—was as good for Judah as Jehoshaphat, Hezekiah, or Josiah, but together they did provide the longest continuous span of God-approved leadership in Judah's history.[3]

Joash died at the hands of assassins; his son Amaziah succeeded him.

3. Thomas L. Constable, "2 Kings," *The Bible Knowledge Commentary*, Old Testament edition, ed. John F. Walvoord and Roy B. Zuck (Wheaton, Ill.: Scripture Press Publications, Victor Books, 1985), p. 561.

The Rest of Israel's and Judah's Kings

Beginning in chapter 13, the narrative shifts into high gear, synopsizing the reigns of kings from both kingdoms.

Jehoahaz of Israel (13:1–9). Because Jehoahaz, Jehu's son, "followed the sins of Jeroboam the son of Nebat" (13:2), God used the Arameans to chastise the Israelites under his reign.

Jehoash of Israel (13:10–13), Jehoahaz' son (also called Joash), also "did evil in the sight of the Lord" (v. 11). Elisha died during his reign, but not before blessing Israel with military victories against the Arameans.

Amaziah of Judah (14:1–14) "did right in the sight of the Lord" (14:3) but failed to eradicate the high places. Amaziah, like his father Joash, was assassinated. His son Azariah succeeded him.

Jeroboam II of Israel (14:23–29). Like his namesake, the first monarch of the northern kingdom, Jeroboam II "did evil in the sight of the Lord" (14:24). God's grace shone clearly, however, allowing him to recover territories held by Israel's enemies.

Azariah of Judah (15:1–7), also called Uzziah, became king at sixteen and reigned fifty-two years—the second longest reign in Judah (Manasseh reigned fifty-five years). He "did right in the sight of the Lord. . . . Only the high places were not taken away" (15:3–4). Second Chronicles tells us that Azariah eventually grew proud and usurped the duties of the priests, for which God struck him with leprosy (2 Chron. 26:16–23).

Zechariah, Shallum, and Menahem of Israel (15:8–22). Zechariah, Jeroboam II's son, ruled only six months before being murdered by Shallum, who reigned only one month before being assassinated by Menahem. An evil, vicious king, Menahem staved off an Assyrian invasion by buying off the king.

Pekahiah and Pekah of Israel (15:23–31). Menahem's son, Pekahiah, continued to lead Israel down the path of evil, until he was murdered by Pekah. Pekah's wicked reign lasted twenty years. The king of Assyria plundered many cities of Israel during his reign, even deporting some Israelites to Assyria.

Jotham of Judah (15:32–38), Azariah's son, completes a grouping of four good kings of Judah.

Ahaz of Judah (16:1–20). Unlike the four kings of Judah before him, Jotham's son, Ahaz, "walked in the way of the kings of Israel" (16:3). He also formed an unhealthy alliance with the king of Assyria, which opened the door for enemy invasion. After his sixteen-year reign, his son Hezekiah succeeded him.

Hoshea: The last king of Israel (17:1–41). Israel's days as a nation came to a close under Hoshea. In 722 B.C. God sent the Assyrians to capture Samaria and carry off her inhabitants because they "had not obeyed the Lord their God, but had violated his covenant— all that Moses the servant of the Lord commanded. They neither listened to the commands nor carried them out" (18:12 NIV; see also 17:7–17). The king of Assyria replaced the population of Israel with other subjugated peoples. He even moved a priest there to teach God's way, therefore appeasing His wrath. But "while these nations feared the Lord, they also served their idols" (17:41).

That's how God judged Israel for her disobedience. Judah's turn would come 136 years later.

Emphasis on the Southern Kingdom (Chaps. 18–25)

With the kingdom of Israel now fallen, the writer of 1 Kings shifts his attention to the final kings of Judah.

Hezekiah (Chaps. 18–20)

Judah's hard road to Babylonian captivity was not without rest stops of spiritual renewal and vitality. King Hezekiah, for example,

> did right in the sight of the Lord, according to all
> that his father David had done. . . . He trusted in
> the Lord, the God of Israel; so that after him there
> was none like him among all the kings of Judah, nor
> among those who were before him. (18:3, 5)

Hezekiah purged the land of idols, including the high places; and his faith in God saved Jerusalem from the Assyrians. As a reward for his dependence on God, the Lord added fifteen years to his life (20:6). An instance of pride, however, when Hezekiah tried to impress some visitors from Babylon, brought a prediction of Babylonian captivity—but not in Hezekiah's lifetime (vv. 12–21).

Manasseh (21:1–18)

What a difference a generation can make! Manasseh may have been the worst king in both Israel and Judah's history. He undid all the good his father, Hezekiah, had done. He rebuilt the high places, revived Baal worship, and erected idols throughout the land. He practiced witchcraft and consulted mediums. He even offered his son as a human sacrifice. His bloody rule lasted longer than any other king of Judah or Israel—fifty-five years.

Amon (21:19–26)

Manasseh's son was no better than his father. He was killed by his own officials.

Josiah (22–23:30)

As Judah's last good king, Josiah led the nation in unprecedented revival. While the temple was being repaired, a priest found a lost copy of the Book of the Law. After hearing it read, young Josiah grieved at how far the people had drifted from God's standards.

So the king made a covenant to follow the Lord. He tore down the idols and got rid of corrupt priests and mediums. Perhaps most importantly, he reinstated the Passover. Josiah died in battle against Pharaoh Neco of Egypt.

> And before him there was no king like him who turned to the Lord with all his heart and with all his soul and with all his might, according to all the law of Moses; nor did any like him arise after him. (23:25)

Jehoahaz, Jehoiakim, Jehoiachin, and Zedekiah (23:31–25:30)

Judah had four more kings over the next twenty-two and a half years before falling to the Babylonians. None of the four walked with the Lord. Jehoahaz died as a prisoner of Pharaoh Neco in Egypt. Under Jehoiakim, Judah was a vassal state of Babylon. But Jehoiakim rebelled against Babylon's king, Nebuchadnezzar, causing the king and several other enemy nations to attack Jerusalem (602 B.C.). Upon Jehoiakim's death, his son, Jehoiachin, took the throne. He was deported to Babylon in 597 B.C.

In 586 B.C., during Zedekiah's reign, Nebuchadnezzar broke through the walls of Jerusalem. The last thing Zedekiah saw was the murder of his sons—after their death, Zedekiah's eyes were gouged out and he was taken away in shackles. Jerusalem was burned, the temple dismantled, and its riches carted off to Babylon.

Thus God's heavy hand of judgment fell on Judah. But He would not forget His people. Even in captivity, He would encourage, protect, and preserve them.

In the thirty-seventh year of the exile of Jehoiachin king of Judah, in the year Evil-Merodach became king of Babylon, he released Jehoiachin from prison. . . . He spoke kindly to him and gave him a seat of honor higher than those of the other kings who were with him in Babylon. So Jehoiachin put aside his prison clothes and for the rest of his life ate regularly at the king's table. Day by day the king gave Jehoiachin a regular allowance as long as he lived. (vv. 27–30 NIV)

Eventually, He would bring them back to Jerusalem.

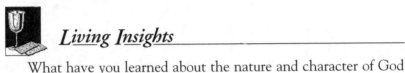

Living Insights

What have you learned about the nature and character of God from your study of the kings of Israel and Judah? Have you discovered again how seriously He views sin? How patient, loving, and merciful He is? How passionately interested He is in the lives of His people? How unfailing His promises are? Record what you have uncovered.

What His prophets teach me: _____

_____

_____

What the evil kings teach me: _____

_____

_____

What the good kings teach me: _____

_____

_____

Do you think God was fair in His final judgment of His people? Why or why not? _____

_____

_____

Chapter 14

1 AND 2 CHRONICLES: REASSURANCE FOR A REMNANT

A Survey of 1 and 2 Chronicles

T hese words, which affirm the identity of God's people, flowed from the apostle Peter's pen. Yet they might just as well have been written by the chronicler to his nation's returned exiles.

> You are a chosen people, a royal priesthood, a holy nation, a people belonging to God, that you may declare the praises of him who called you out of darkness into his wonderful light. Once you were not a people, but now you are the people of God; once you had not received mercy, but now you have received mercy. (1 Pet. 2:9–10 NIV)

Having passed through a terrible seventy years of God's judgment due to their sins, the Jews must have had their doubts about their future. Would God still want to keep His covenants with their feeble, diminished nation? Did He still have a plan--"a future and a hope"—for them (Jer. 29:11)? After they had betrayed His love and kindness, could He still have a purpose for them? Were they still His people?

Yes, the chronicler would answer, you are still "a chosen people, a royal priesthood, a holy nation, a people belonging to God." To this remnant of hopeful, hesitant Hebrews, the chronicler offers the reassurance of God's grace and irrevocable call (see Rom. 11, note especially v. 29).

Keys to Understanding and Appreciating the Chronicles

The books of Chronicles cover the same period of Jewish history described in 2 Samuel through 2 Kings. But they are much more than a rehash. Beginning with Adam, 1 Chronicles traces God's choosing of a people, then a specific tribe, then one man's line through whom God's Messiah would save and bless the world.

1 AND 2 CHRONICLES

1 Chronicles
God's View: Chosen

2 Chronicles
. . . and Preserved

	GENEALOGIES	SAUL	DAVID AND THE TEMPLE	SOLOMON The King	JUDAH The Nation REVIVAL / REJECTION
	CHAPTERS 1–9	CHAPTER 10	CHAPTERS 11–29	CHAPTERS 1–9	CHAPTERS 10–36

CONSECRATION — Glory — RESTORATION

Process	Little made great	Great becoming little
Emphasis	Personal determination	National deterioration
History	Creation of world to creation of kingdom	Solomon's temple to rebuilding of temple
Unifying Theme	The temple — the structural state of the temple corresponds to the spiritual state of the people	
Key Passages	1 Chronicles 17; 29:10–22; 2 Chronicles 7:12–22; 16:9a	
Christ in Chronicles	Christ is foretold in the Davidic Covenant (1 Chron. 17) and prefigured in the idealized kings David and Solomon; also the ark and the temple typify Christ's power and presence with us	

Second Chronicles reiterates God's faithfulness in spite of His people's faithlessness and illustrates the hope of restoration in spite of His people's rebellion.

The books of Chronicles, more than anything else, present the sweep and essence of salvation history.

The Name and Biblical Order

First and 2 Chronicles, like Samuel and Kings, were originally one book. The Hebrew title, *dibre hayyamim*, means "the events (or annals) of the days (or years)." The Greek Septuagint mistakenly classified it as a supplement to Samuel and Kings, titling it "The Things Omitted." Jerome (A.D. 347–420) in translating the Scriptures into Latin, suggested a more fitting name: "chronicle of the whole sacred history."[1]

In our present-day Bible, 1 and 2 Chronicles precede the books that continue their story—Ezra and Nehemiah. However, the Hebrew Scriptures conclude with the Chronicles. Michael Wilcock highlights the significance of this.

> The way the Chronicler summarizes [old fundamental] truths, teaching nothing which could not be found elsewhere in Scripture, yet teaching with a sense of vividness, contrast, and drama which are all his own, must recall the last book of the New Testament. Like John and Revelation, Chronicles rounds off an entire major section of Scripture by saying, "This is what it is really all about. This is what it has always been about, what it always will be about."[2]

The Author and Historical Setting

Jewish tradition names Ezra as the author, but no writer is named in the books. For that reason, we'll refer to the writer as "the chronicler," allowing room for Ezra's authorship or that of a contemporary of his.

Probably completed between 450 and 400 B.C., the Chronicles

---

1. Raymond Dillard, "Introduction to 1 Chronicles," in *The NIV Study Bible*, ed. Kenneth Barker and others (Grand Rapids, Mich.: Zondervan Publishing House, 1985), p. 578.

2. Michael Wilcock, *The Message of Chronicles*, The Bible Speaks Today Series (Downers Grove, Ill.: InterVarsity Press, 1987), p. 18.

spoke to the Jews who had returned to their homeland after the Babylonian exile. The temple would have already been rebuilt, around 516 B.C., and Nehemiah might have finished rebuilding Jerusalem's wall by this time. This community, then, would have been trying to get back on their feet as the people of God.

The Uniqueness of the Chronicles

Because the writers had different purposes, Chronicles is more positive than Samuel and Kings. For example, the chronicler omits David's sin with Bathsheba and the ensuing turmoil in his family and the nation. Solomon's sins are omitted too; instead, his building of the temple takes precedence. Also, you won't find Israel's history here—just Judah's—because the northern kingdom abandoned the Lord's temple to worship idols. They weren't abandoned by God, however; Judah repeatedly invited the northern tribes to join in their reforms and revivals, and many did. Finally, of the twenty-seven chapters dealing with Judah's kings, nineteen are devoted to the eight "good" monarchs.

The following chart helps crystallize the Chronicles' uniqueness.[3]

Samuel and Kings	Chronicles
• Israel's history from united kingdom to two captivities	• Focuses on Judah's Davidic line through exile to decree to return
• Written soon after the events	• Written long after the events
• More negative—rebellion and tragedy	• More positive—apostasy, but hope in spite of tragedy
• Message of judgment	• Message of hope
• Man's failings	• God's faithfulness
• Emphasizes kings and prophets	• Emphasizes temple and priests

The Purpose and Themes

In writing his perspective on the Jews' history, the chronicler sought to encourage his people that God was still with them, just as He had always been—that there was continuity between their

3. Adapted from Bruce Wilkinson and Kenneth Boa, *Talk Thru the Old Testament*, vol. 1 of *Talk Thru the Bible* (Nashville, Tenn.: Thomas Nelson Publishers, 1983), p. 102.

glorious past and their struggling present. Eugene Merrill gets even more specific:

> The purpose of 1 and 2 Chronicles is to show God's elective and preserving grace in His covenant people through David, the messianic king and priest.[4]

With such a grand purpose as this, it's no wonder these two books are rich in themes. Here are just a few:

- God sovereignly elects, shaping history to accomplish His good will.

- When we oppose God through disobedience, we experience judgment. But when we repent and humbly seek Him, He forgives and restores.

- God honors a heart that is wholly His.

Overview of the Chronicles

Now that we possess the keys to understanding the Chronicles, let's unlock the treasures in the books' four major sections.

God's Chosen People (1 Chron. 1–9)

"What could be more stupendously dull than the first nine chapters of 1 Chronicles?" commentator Michael Wilcock facetiously asks.[5] And they are daunting: page after page of names, with obscure historical tidbits sprinkled in here and there. Nevertheless, there's a pattern here, and we'll be richer for seeing it.

Chapters 1–3, in moving from Adam to "the sons of Elioenai," trace creation to restoration. These genealogies show God choosing His own people (in Abraham); His own nation (in Jacob, called Israel in these books); His kingly tribe (in Judah); and His kingly, messianic line (in David). In tracing David's line past the exile and into the restoration, the author emphasizes the continuity of God's people and His covenant.

Chapters 4–7 follow the tribes of Israel, with special emphasis

4. Merrill cites 1 Chronicles 15:25–28 and 2 Samuel 6:12–15 in support of David's priesthood. In these passages, Scripture tells us that he wore a linen ephod, which was a priestly garment. "1 Chronicles," in *The Bible Knowledge Commentary*, Old Testament edition, ed. John F. Walvoord and Roy B. Zuck (Wheaton, Ill.: Scripture Press Publications, Victor Books, 1985), p. 591.

5. Wilcock, *The Message of Chronicles*, p. 19.

on Levi because it was consecrated as the priestly tribe that would guide the people in serving God.[6] Chapter 8 outlines Saul's genealogy through the tribe of Benjamin. Chapter 9 begins by listing the first people to resettle in Jerusalem after the exile; then it ends by repeating Saul's genealogy—a prelude to chapter 10.

God's Chosen King (1 Chron. 10–29)

Saul's death and a brief commentary on his unfaithfulness serve as a transition to David's faithful reign (chap. 10). Starting with all Israel anointing David king in Hebron (11:1–3), the chronicler moves swiftly through David's conquest of Jerusalem, the tales and roster of his mighty men, and a list of his warriors (11:4–12:40). These two chapters paint a picture of unity and joy in Israel.

David next sought out the ark of God, which had been neglected in Saul's reign. David didn't handle it the way God commanded, however, and a man died as a result. Afraid of the Lord's anger, David returned to his own house, having left the ark with Obed-edom (chap. 13). Chapter 14 records an interlude in which David's palace, family, and nation were built up; then the chronicler returns to his focus: the ark. At last, following the law's instruction, David joyfully brought the ark to Jerusalem and composed a psalm praising God's might and glory (chaps. 15–16).

Not satisfied merely to bring the ark to Jerusalem, David next wanted to glorify God by building a temple to house it. God, however, had something else in mind.

> "Go and tell David My servant, 'Thus says the Lord, "You shall not build a house for Me to dwell in. . . . Moreover, I tell you that the Lord will build a house [i.e., dynasty] for you. And it shall come about when your days are fulfilled that you must go to be with your fathers, that I will set up one of your descendants after you, who shall be of your sons; and I will establish his kingdom. He shall build for Me a house, and I will establish his throne forever. I will be his father, and he shall be My son; and I will not take My lovingkindness away from him, as I took it

---

6. The chronicler focuses on the temple, the Levites, and priests probably because, without a Davidic king to guide the recovering nation, the priests and Levites would serve a crucial role in leading the remnant.

from him who was before you. But I will settle him in My house and in My kingdom forever, and his throne shall be established forever.""" (17:4, 10b–14)

Not only would David's son have the honor of building the Lord's temple, but David's line would be honored by being settled in *the Lord's house and kingdom forever.* This pledge is known as the Davidic covenant, its messianic promise pointing to a future Son, Jesus Christ. Deeply moved by God's grace, David responds in prayer (17:16–27).

As if to prove God's blessing on David, chapters 18–20 proclaim his victories in battle. Chapter 21, however, swerves in another direction, recounting David's sin of taking a census. Significantly, when we track the story to its conclusion in 22:1, we find that it has led us to the temple—specifically, the site where the temple would be built. Continuing with this new temple theme, chapters 22–26 show David preparing the temple's building materials and determining the service of the Levites, priests, singers, gatekeepers, treasurers, and other temple officials. Chapter 27 interrupts with a list of army divisions and the king's overseers; then we're back on track with the temple plans, which include David's and the people's gifts for its sacred articles (chaps. 28:1–29:9).

In the final section of 1 Chronicles, David praises God for allowing them to complete the temple preparations, and he asks the Lord to keep the nation's and his son Solomon's hearts devoted to Him. Solomon is then anointed king, and David dies in peace.

God's Chosen Son (2 Chron. 1–9)

The chronicler's account of Solomon's life focuses predominantly on his building of the temple. In chapter 1, God grants Solomon's request for wisdom and adds the splendor that no king of Israel would ever match. Then chapters 2–7 concentrate on the temple: chapter 2 details Solomon's additional preparations; chapter 3 depicts the temple's construction; chapter 4 lists its furnishings; chapter 5 places the ark in the Holy of Holies; chapter 6 records Solomon's praise and prayer of dedication; and chapter 7 tells of the sacrifices of dedication and the two weeks of celebration.

The latter half of chapter 7 records the Lord's response to Solomon's prayer, which contains the first key passage of 2 Chronicles:

"[If] My people who are called by My name humble themselves and pray, and seek My face and turn from their wicked ways, then will I hear from heaven, will forgive their sin, and will heal their land. Now My eyes shall be open and My ears attentive to the prayer offered in this place. For now I have chosen and consecrated this house that My name may be there forever, and My eyes and My heart will be there perpetually." (vv. 14–16)

As we'll see in the rest of 2 Chronicles, the Lord kept His word to those who humbled themselves and repented. What an encouragement this theme must have been to the remnant who had recently emerged from God's punishment.

Chapters 8 and 9 sum up Solomon's other activities—the building of his palace, the Queen of Sheba's visit, and how Solomon made "silver as common as stones in Jerusalem" (9:27). Interestingly, when his death is recorded, there is not a single mention of his sins.

God's Chosen Dynasty (2 Chron. 10–36)

From the wisdom of Solomon we come to the foolishness of his son Rehoboam in chapter 10. Here Rehoboam's harsh rule splits the kingdom. But God preserves David's dynasty in the southern kingdom,[7] which the chronicler traces throughout the rest of his book.

Chapters 10–11 show Rehoboam initially following the Lord, then falling away, and finally humbling himself before God. The Lord turned His anger away and preserved Jerusalem, but Solomon's glorious temple was plundered—the golden gifts of David's and Solomon's generations replaced with bronze. After Rehoboam's death, his son Abijah (Abijam in 1 Kings) took the throne. He is remembered by the writer as one who stood for God against idolatrous Jeroboam. No moral judgment—either good or bad—follows the account of his reign (chap. 13).

The next seven chapters tell the stories of Judah's first two reformers, Asa and his son Jehoshaphat (chaps. 14–20). Though not always following the Lord perfectly, these two monarchs gave Judah sixty-six years of peace and obedience to God. In Asa's story we find the second key verse of 2 Chronicles:

7. Notice that the priests and Levites, God's representatives, sided with Rehoboam (11:13–17).

"For the eyes of the Lord move to and fro throughout the earth that He may strongly support those whose heart is completely His." (16:9a)

If only they would have believed God's word.

Chapter 21 brings us to Jehoshaphat's son Jehoram. Marrying a daughter of the infamous Ahab, Athaliah, this murderous king was rebuked by Israel's prophet Elijah and told that he would die in great pain. God preserved his life solely for the sake of the promise He made to David, but Jehoram's disobedience led to his disease and finally to disgrace. His son Ahaziah was no better, and when he died, his mother, Queen Athaliah, tried to destroy David's dynasty (chap. 22).

A priest named Jehoiada managed to overthrow the queen after six years, putting the rightful heir, young Joash, on the throne. The Davidic dynasty and messianic line were preserved through him, and while his mentor Jehoiada was alive, he walked with God (chap. 23). In chapter 24, we find that he repaired the temple and reformed the land; but after Jehoiada's death, he let his heart for God go to ruins. His son Amaziah followed God initially, but then he, too, fell away to idols (chap. 25). Uzziah, his son, was a good king who walked with God and prospered for a long time. However, his pride brought his downfall, and his son Jotham ruled in his place (chap. 26). Jotham was the last good king Judah would have for the next sixteen years (chap. 27).

The unfaithful, idolatrous reign of Jotham's son Ahaz shaped the land next, finally giving way to one of Judah's greatest kings, Ahaz's son Hezekiah (chap. 28).

The chronicler devotes most of the next four chapters to all the good Hezekiah did. He purified the temple, repairing the damage from the previous reign (chap. 29); celebrated the Passover, inviting the northern tribes to join Judah (chap. 30); provided for the temple worship (chap. 31); and defeated Assyria's king when he attacked Judah (chap. 32). His reign was likened to David's, but his son's reign set a new standard for wickedness.

In chapter 33, Judah's most wicked king, Manasseh, takes the throne. The chronicler, however, devotes as much space to his repentance as he does to his evil. When Manasseh humbled himself before God, the Lord listened even to him. But, the tide of the nation's idolatry was not stemmed by their king's repentance. His son Amon was next on the throne, and his brief, evil reign merited only five verses (33:21–25).

With Josiah, however, Judah had her last glimmer of glory. Though Amon's son, Josiah, was a righteous young man, taking the throne when he was only eight years old. He sought the Lord, purged the land of its false gods, restored the temple, and rediscovered God's law (chap. 34). He also celebrated a Passover like none other since the days of Samuel (chap. 35). When he died, the lamp of Judah flickered and dimmed.

In rapid fashion in chapter 36, the chronicler records the last four unfaithful kings of Judah, the fall of Jerusalem, and the exile. He explains that while Judah was in Babylon, the Lord's land finally had the sabbath rests the people had denied it. But the book doesn't end there.

Second Chronicles concludes with the Lord moving a pagan king's heart, Cyrus of Persia, to let His people return to Jerusalem and Judah—to rebuild God's temple and their relationship with Him.

From Solomon's temple to the decree to rebuild it, 2 Chronicles shows that God is with His people through all generations.

----◆----

The Lord set his affection on your forefathers and loved them, and he chose you, their descendants, above all the nations, as it is today. (Deut. 10:15 NIV)

 Living Insights

Have you ever done something that you felt sure God could not—would not want to—forgive? That He was disgusted with you, and that you were beyond His care? If so, 1 and 2 Chronicles are for you.

These books tell the story of God choosing and loving and blessing a people He would call His own, only to have those people despise Him, desert Him, disobey His righteous and merciful laws, and dishonor His holy name. Yet, even though He had to discipline them through exile, He reassured them that they were His own—that they would always be His own. And that He wanted to be with them still.

Are you still a little unsure? Then gather some strength from the chronicler's reassurance.

2 Chron. 6:36–39; 7:12–16 _____

_____

_____

2 Chron. 12:5–8 _____

_____

_____

2 Chron. 30:6–9 _____

_____

_____

2 Chron. 33:10–13 _____

_____

_____

2 Chron. 36:15–23 _____

_____

_____

For further study in the richness of 1 and 2 Chronicles, we highly recommend Michael Wilcock's *The Message of Chronicles*, The Bible Speaks Today Series (Downers Grove, Ill.: InterVarsity Press, 1987).

BOOKS FOR PROBING FURTHER

B ravo! You've taken in the themes and nuances of this first movement of God's symphony of Scripture. For further reflection on the recurring motifs in Genesis through 2 Chronicles, we recommend the following excellent resources.

Baxter, J. Sidlow. *Explore the Book*. Grand Rapids, Mich.: Zondervan Publishing House, Academie Books, 1960.

Blaiklock, E. M. *Today's Handbook of Bible Characters*. Minneapolis, Minn.: Bethany House Publishers, 1979.

Bright, John. *A History of Israel*. 3d ed. Philadelphia, Pa.: Westminster Press, 1981.

Clowney, Edmund P. *The Unfolding Mystery: Discovering Christ in the Old Testament*. Colorado Springs, Colo.: NavPress, 1988.

Geisler, Norman L., and William E. Nix. *A General Introduction to the Bible*. Rev. ed. Chicago, Ill.: Moody Press, 1986.

Lee-Thorp, Karen. *The Story of Stories*. Rev. ed. Colorado Springs, Colo.: NavPress, 1995.

Walvoord, John F., and Roy B. Zuck, eds. *The Bible Knowledge Commentary*. Old Testament edition. Wheaton, Ill.: Scripture Press Publications, Victor Books, 1985.

Wilkinson, Bruce, and Kenneth Boa. *Talk Thru the Bible*. Nashville, Tenn.: Thomas Nelson Publishers, 1983.

Some of these books may be out of print and available only through a library. For those currently available, please contact your local Christian bookstore. Books by Charles R. Swindoll may be obtained through Insight for Living. IFL also offers some books by other authors—please note the ordering information that follows and contact the office that serves you.

ORDERING INFORMATION

GOD'S MASTERWORK
Volume One
Cassette Tapes and Study Guide

This Bible study guide was designed to be used independently or in conjunction with the broadcast of Chuck Swindoll's taped messages which are listed below. If you would like to order cassette tapes or further copies of this study guide, please see the information given below and the order form provided at the end of this guide.

		U.S.	Canada
GM1	Study guide	$ 4.95	$ 6.50
GM1CS	Cassette series, includes all individual tapes, album cover, and one complimentary study guide	46.75	53.75
GM1 1–7	Individual cassettes, includes messages A and B	6.00	7.48

Prices are subject to change without notice.

GM1 1-A: *A Symphony for the Soul*—Selected Scriptures
      B: *Genesis: Where It All Begins*—A Survey of Genesis

GM1 2-A: *Exodus: Story of Miraculous Freedom*—A Survey of Exodus
      B: *Leviticus: God's Picture Book on Worship*—A Survey of Leviticus

GM1 3-A: *Numbers: A Tragic Pilgrimage*—A Survey of Numbers
      B: *Deuteronomy: Remember! Remember!*—A Survey of Deuteronomy

GM1 4-A: *Joshua: Triumph after Tragedy*—A Survey of Joshua
      B: *Judges: Recycled Misery*—A Survey of Judges

GM1 5-A: *Ruth: Interlude of Love*—A Survey of Ruth
      B: *1 Samuel: Nation in Transition*—A Survey of 1 Samuel

GM1 6-A: *2 Samuel: Ecstasy and Agony of a King*—A Survey of 2 Samuel
      B: *1 Kings: Solomon and a Civil War*—A Survey of 1 Kings

GM1 7-A: *2 Kings: From Compromise to Captivity*—A Survey of
       2 Kings
     B: *1 and 2 Chronicles: Reassurance for a Remnant*—
       A Survey of 1 and 2 Chronicles

HOW TO ORDER BY PHONE OR FAX
(Credit card orders only)

Web site: http://www.insight.org

United States: 1-800-772-8888 or FAX (714) 575-5684, 24 hours a day,
7 days a week

Canada: 1-800-663-7639 or FAX (604) 532-7173, 24 hours a day, 7 days
a week

Australia and the South Pacific: (03) 9872-4606 from 8:00 A.M. to
5:00 P.M., Monday through Friday.
FAX (03) 9874-8890 anytime, day or night

Other International Locations: call the International Ordering Services
Department in the United States at (714) 575-5000 from 8:00 A.M.
to 4:30 P.M., Pacific time, Monday through Friday
FAX (714) 575-5683 anytime, day or night

HOW TO ORDER BY MAIL

United States
- Mail to: Mail Center
  Insight for Living
  Post Office Box 69000
  Anaheim, CA 92817-0900
- Sales tax: California residents add 7.75%.
- Shipping and handling charges must be added to each order. See chart
on order form for amount.
- Payment: personal checks, money orders, credit cards (Visa, MasterCard,
Discover Card, and American Express). No invoices or COD orders available.
- $10 fee for *any* returned check.

Canada
- Mail to: Insight for Living Ministries
  Post Office Box 2510
  Vancouver, BC V6B 3W7
- Sales tax: please add 7% GST. British Columbia residents also add 7%
sales tax (on tapes or cassette series).

- Shipping and handling charges must be added to each order. See chart on order form for amount.
- Payment: personal cheques, money orders, credit cards (Visa, Master-Card). No invoices or COD orders available.
- Delivery: approximately four weeks.

Australia and the South Pacific
- Mail to: Insight for Living, Inc.
  GPO Box 2823 EE
  Melbourne, Victoria 3001, Australia
- Shipping: add 25% to the total order.
- Delivery: approximately four to six weeks.
- Payment: personal checks payable in Australian funds, international money orders, or credit cards (Visa, MasterCard, and Bankcard).

United Kingdom and Europe
- Mail to: Insight for Living
  c/o Trans World Radio
  Post Office Box 1020
  Bristol BS99 1XS
  England, United Kingdom
- Shipping: add 25% to the total order.
- Delivery: approximately four to six weeks.
- Payment: cheques payable in sterling pounds or credit cards (Visa, MasterCard, and American Express).

Other International Locations
- Mail to: International Processing Services Department
  Insight for Living
  Post Office Box 69000
  Anaheim, CA 92817-0900
- Shipping and delivery time: please see chart that follows.
- Payment: personal checks payable in U.S. funds, international money orders, or credit cards (Visa, MasterCard, and American Express).

Type of Shipping	Postage Cost	Delivery
Surface	10% of total order*	6 to 10 weeks
Airmail	25% of total order*	under 6 weeks

Use U.S. price as a base.

Our Guarantee: Your complete satisfaction is our top priority here at Insight for Living. If you're not completely satisfied with anything you order, please return it for full credit, a refund, or a replacement, as you prefer.

Insight for Living Catalog: The Insight for Living catalog features study guides, tapes, and books by a variety of Christian authors. To obtain a free copy, call us at the numbers listed above.

Order Form
United States, Australia, and Other International Locations
(Canadian residents please use order form on reverse side.)

GM1CS represents the entire *God's Masterwork, Volume One* series in a special album cover, while GM1 1–7 are the individual tapes included in the series. GM1 represents this study guide, should you desire to order additional copies.

Product Code	Product Description	Qty	Price	Total
GM1	Study Guide		$ 4.95	$
GM1CS	Casette Series with study guide		46.75	
GM1- ☐	Individual cassette		6.00	
GM1- ☐	Individual cassette		6.00	
GM1- ☐	Individual cassette		6.00	

Order Total

UPS ☐   First Class ☐
*Shipping and handling must be added.
See chart for charges.*

Amount of Order	First Class	UPS
$ 7.50 and under	1.00	4.00
$ 7.51 to 12.50	1.50	4.25
$12.51 to 25.00	3.50	4.50
$25.01 to 35.00	4.50	4.75
$35.01 to 60.00	5.50	5.25
$60.00 to 99.99	6.50	5.75
$100.00 and over	No Charge	

Rush shipping and Fourth Class are also available. Please call for details.

Subtotal

California Residents—Sales Tax
Add 7.75% of subtotal.

Non-United States Residents
*Australia and Europe: add 25%.
Other: Price +10% surface or 25% airmail.*

Gift to Insight for Living
Tax-deductible in the United States.

Total Amount Due $
Please do not send cash.

Prices are subject to change without notice.

Payment by: ☐ Check or money order payable to Insight for Living or
☐ Visa   ☐ MasterCard   ☐ Discover Card   ☐ American Express   ☐ Bankcard
(In Australia)

Number |

Expiration Date | | / | | Signature
We cannot process your credit card purchase without your signature

Name:
Address:
City: State:
Zip Code: Country:
Telephone: (   )   –   Radio Station:

If questions arise concerning your order, we may need to contact you.

Mail this order form to the Mail Center at one of these addresses:

Insight for Living
Post Office Box 69000, Anaheim, CA 92817-0900

Insight for Living, Inc.
GPO Box 2823 EE, Melbourne, VIC 3001, Australia

Order Form
Canadian Residents
(Residents of the United States, Australia, and other international locations, please use order form on reverse side.)

GM1CS represents the entire *God's Masterwork, Volume One* series in a special album cover, while GM1 1–7 are the individual tapes included in the series. GM1 represents this study guide, should you desire to order additional copies.

Product Code	Product Description	Qty	Price	Total
GM1	Study Guide		$ 6.50	$
GM1CS	Casette Series with study guide		53.75	
GM1- ☐	Individual cassette		7.48	
GM1- ☐	Individual cassette		7.48	
GM1- ☐	Individual cassette		7.48	

Amount of Order	Canada Post
Orders to $10.00	2.00
$10.01 to 30.00	3.50
$30.01 to 50.00	5.00
$50.01 to 99.99	7.00
$100 and over	No charge

Loomis Courier is also available.
Please call for details.

Subtotal

Add 7% GST
British Columbia Residents
Add 7% sales tax on individual tapes or cassette series.

Shipping
Shipping and Handling must be added.
See chart for charges.

Gift to Insight for Living Ministries
Tax-deductible in Canada.

Total Amount Due $
Please do not send cash.

Prices are subject to change without notice.

Payment by: ☐ Cheque or money order payable to Insight for Living Ministries or
☐ Visa ☐ MasterCard

Number

Expiration Date ☐☐/☐☐ Signature
We cannot process your credit card purchase without your signature.

Name:

Address:

City: Province:

Postal Code: Country:

Telephone: ( ) – Radio Station:

If questions arise concerning your order, we may need to contact you.

Mail this order form to the Processing Services Department at the following address:

Insight for Living Ministries
Post Office Box 2510
Vancouver, BC, Canada V6B 3W7

Order Form
United States, Australia, and Other International Locations
(Canadian residents please use order form on reverse side.)

GM1CS represents the entire *God's Masterwork, Volume One* series in a special album cover, while GM1 1–7 are the individual tapes included in the series. GM1 represents this study guide, should you desire to order additional copies.

Product Code	Product Description	Qty	Price	Total
GM1	Study Guide		$ 4.95	$
GM1CS	Casette Series with study guide		46.75	
GM1- ☐	Individual cassette		6.00	
GM1- ☐	Individual cassette		6.00	
GM1- ☐	Individual cassette		6.00	

Order Total

UPS ☐ **First Class** ☐
Shipping and handling must be added.
See chart for charges.

Amount of Order	First Class	UPS
$ 7.50 and under	1.00	4.00
$ 7.51 to 12.50	1.50	4.25
$12.51 to 25.00	3.50	4.50
$25.01 to 35.00	4.50	4.75
$35.01 to 60.00	5.50	5.25
$60.00 to 99.99	6.50	5.75
$100.00 and over	No Charge	

Rush shipping and Fourth Class are also available. Please call for details.

Subtotal

California Residents—Sales Tax
Add 7.75% of subtotal.

Non-United States Residents
Australia and Europe: add 25%.
Other: Price +10% surface or 25% airmail.

Gift to Insight for Living
Tax-deductible in the United States.

Total Amount Due $
Please do not send cash.

Prices are subject to change without notice.

Payment by: ☐ Check or money order payable to Insight for Living or
☐ Visa ☐ MasterCard ☐ Discover Card ☐ American Express ☐ Bankcard
(In Australia)

Number

Expiration Date ☐☐/☐☐ Signature
We cannot process your credit card purchase without your signature

Name:

Address:

City: State:

Zip Code: Country:

Telephone: ( ) – Radio Station:

If questions arise concerning your order, we may need to contact you.

Mail this order form to the Mail Center at one of these addresses:

Insight for Living
Post Office Box 69000, Anaheim, CA 92817-0900

Insight for Living, Inc.
GPO Box 2823 EE, Melbourne, VIC 3001, Australia

Order Form
Canadian Residents
(Residents of the United States, Australia, and other international locations,
please use order form on reverse side.)

GM1CS represents the entire *God's Masterwork, Volume One* series in a special album cover,
while GM1 1–7 are the individual tapes included in the series. GM1 represents this study guide,
should you desire to order additional copies.

Product Code	Product Description	Qty	Price	Total
GM1	Study Guide		$ 6.50	$
GM1CS	Casette Series with study guide		53.75	
GM1- ☐	Individual cassette		7.48	
GM1- ☐	Individual cassette		7.48	
GM1- ☐	Individual cassette		7.48	

Amount of Order	Canada Post
Orders to $10.00	2.00
$10.01 to 30.00	3.50
$30.01 to 50.00	5.00
$50.01 to 99.99	7.00
$100 and over	No charge

Loomis Courier is also available.
Please call for details.

Subtotal

Add 7% GST
British Columbia Residents
*Add 7% sales tax on
individual tapes or cassette series.*

Shipping
*Shipping and Handling must be added.
See chart for charges.*

Gift to Insight for Living Ministries
Tax-deductible in Canada.

Total Amount Due $
Please do not send cash.

Prices are subject to change without notice.

Payment by: ☐ Cheque or money order payable to Insight for Living Ministries or
☐ Visa ☐ MasterCard

Number

Expiration Date ☐ ☐ / ☐ ☐ Signature
We cannot process your credit card purchase without your signature.

Name:
Address:
City: Province:
Postal Code: Country:
Telephone: ( ) – Radio Station:

If questions arise concerning your order, we may need to contact you.

Mail this order form to the Processing Services Department at the following address:

Insight for Living Ministries
Post Office Box 2510
Vancouver, BC, Canada V6B 3W7